BAKE AMERICA GREAT AGAIN

★ ★ ★

BAKE AMERICA GREAT AGAIN

★ ★ ★

*50 Sweet Recipes
to Make a Difference*

Amber Gentry **and** Kirsten Hall

≡Bluestreak

⇛Bluestreak

An imprint of Weldon Owen

1045 Sansome Street, Suite 100, San Francisco, CA 94111

www.weldonowen.com

Weldon Owen is a division of Bonnier Publishing USA

ISBN: 978-1-68188-321-2

First Printed in 2017

10 9 8 7 6 5 4 3 2 1

2017 2018 2019 2020

Printed in China

Developed by The Book Shop, Ltd.

Designed by Christine Kettner

Edited by Susan Lauzau

Contents

CHAPTER 3

Sweet Land of Liberty 56

CHAPTER 4

America's Bread Winners— and Muffins and Cakes, Too! 78

CHAPTER 5

Freedom Fighters 100

Dear Readers and Bakers,

First, we want to thank you for buying our book, and we hope you enjoy making some (or all) of the treats we've included. We have worked hard to ensure that the recipes in this book speak to many different tastes and dietary needs.

Second, we want to share a little bit about why we cooked up this book in the first place. For starters, we are truly proud to be Americans, citizens of this great nation built on welcoming all. We believe that each of us has a role to play in keeping our country "great," and we eagerly want to be active participants.

These have been tumultuous times, politically speaking, and we want to be clear that this book is for everyone—it's 100 percent bipartisan! But when we saw the liberties of our friends and fellow citizens endangered recently, we felt we must respond. Watching the rights of people we care about threatened, we were moved to speak up for what we believe in. We asked ourselves, and each other, "What can we do to stand up for equal rights and respect for all people?"

Maybe you have been in that same place. Maybe there has been a moment in which you felt moved to make a difference in your neighborhood or take a stand for something but felt stumped as to how to go about it or discouraged that your effort may not be enough to create change. Trust us, we felt that way, too.

We decided to start small so we weren't intimidated. We chose to hold a bake sale and donate the proceeds to an organization that was helping people in need, and we approached our sale with the same fervor that we give to our most important projects. We trusted that some of our friends would want to help us (and, of course, they did). And with each new recipe signee and friend who joined our effort, we grew more confident that we could fight for what was important to us, that we truly could make a difference.

We struggled to find a space that would host our bake sale (we hadn't realized there would be so many building permissions and regulatory roadblocks in our way). Luckily, at the eleventh hour, we reached out to a space we should have thought of from the very start—a beloved independent children's bookstore. Just as America, in her best moments, traditionally welcomed all the peoples of the world, the store welcomed us immediately and warmly. They said they'd love to support us! And just like that, with the bookstore's generosity, our bake sale was on.

That's when we began searching online for recipes and sifting through our own family favorites. We brainstormed ways we could tweak and rename our recipes to be on brand with our event. We bought and made patriotic decorations (balloons and flags and stickers) and dressed up the space so it would feel friendly and fun. We stayed up late for several nights in a row—bring on the coffee!—baking, icing, packaging, and e-mailing. We tasted cookies, brownies, breads, muffins, scones, and tortes. Each sweet bite brought increased pride and confidence. Our bake sale was not only on, we knew it was destined to be a hit!

And it was. We were amazed by the response of our friends, family, neighbors, and even strangers passing by our bake sale. Everyone was incredibly supportive. So many people donated, often far more than a single cookie is worth. But they weren't just buying a cookie, were they? They were giving to something great. They were giving from the heart and to a cause. They were giving in accordance with their values and showing their conviction for what this country means to them. They were giving to see their ideals and dreams for our nation maintained and carried into the future. They knew that maybe they couldn't write public policy or argue in court, but dang it, they could buy a cookie! And by doing so, they could support those who have the skills to help preserve and protect our liberties.

As we witnessed what was happening, we knew we had tapped into something bigger than ourselves. Bigger than baking. This was a display of the true greatness of America. All of us—of different races, ages, genders, orientations, ideas, and economic strata—can with passion and effort work together toward the same cause: liberty and justice for all.

What if we all gave ourselves to this cause of liberty? What if we didn't worry whether we were big enough to make a difference, but instead trusted that we could create change in the small ways we know how. Our bake sale wound up raising far more than we had hoped, and we donated 100 percent of the proceeds to the ACLU.

We share our story in the hope that it will encourage you to do what we did, to bake for a cause you believe in, if you can't legislate or aren't equipped to "do more." We saw through our bake sale what is possible. And we know you can do this. We can do this. Let's Bake America Great Again!

Love, *Amber & Kirsten*

Guide to Better Baking

★ First, read through the entire recipe before beginning, to make sure that you understand the instructions and that you have the ingredients and equipment you need on hand.

★ Find your tools and measure ingredients before you start. This will allow you to move smoothly from step to step without melted ingredients hardening or chilled ingredients becoming too warm.

★ Measure carefully. Spoon dry ingredients into the measuring cup and then level with the straight edge of a butter knife. Level dry ingredients in measuring spoons as well. For the greatest accuracy, measure liquids in a glass measuring cup and set it on a level surface; bend to eye level to read the measurement.

★ Pay attention to timing. Plan appropriately for butter, eggs, or other ingredients to warm to room temperature, if applicable, or for dough to chill or yeast dough to rise.

★ Place the oven rack in the middle position unless the recipe instructs otherwise. Midway through the baking time, rotate pans from front to back. If appropriate, rotate them from upper to lower rack as well.

★ Use a pan of the correct size. While a pan that is only an inch off may seem similar enough in size, the baking results can be quite different. A 9-inch pan is 25 percent larger than an 8-inch pan, for example. The standard-size muffin pan called for in these recipes has a ½-cup (4-fl oz/125-ml) capacity.

★ Make sure to preheat the oven as directed in the recipe; consider purchasing an oven thermometer to check that your oven's interior temperature matches that of the dial setting.

★ Always start with clean bowls, pans, and beaters. This is particularly critical when whipping egg whites, as fats or yolk left on surfaces can affect the consistency of the whipped whites.

★ Melting chocolate—especially white chocolate—can be tricky. Melt chocolate in the top of a double boiler or in a stainless steel bowl set over a pan of barely simmering water. It is important that no water or moisture gets into the chocolate, or it will "seize" and turn grainy. Stir frequently and take the chocolate off the heat just before it is completely melted—milk chocolate and white chocolate are even more delicate than dark chocolate, and you may have greater success if you turn the heat off just before you add the chocolate to the bowl. The residual heat will melt the chocolate without scorching or causing it to seize.

The Well-Stocked Baker

For the recipes in this book, you will need some basic baking equipment as well as a few specialty tools—though many of these are optional.

Measuring cups and spoons

Mixing bowls in assorted sizes

Microwave-safe bowls

Double boiler or stainless steel bowl and pot

Electric mixer, either hand-held or a stand mixer

Food processor

Wooden spoons

Rolling pin

Ruler

Rubber spatula

Metal spatula

Metal offset spatula and/or spreaders

Chef's knife

Pastry brush

Pastry blender or two knives

Parchment paper or silicone mat

Baking sheets

Cupcake/muffin pans

Baking pans in various sizes

Loaf pan

Wire racks

Pastry bag and decorative tips

Paper or foil cupcake liners

Cookie cutters in various shapes and sizes

Candy thermometer

CHAPTER 1

United Cookies of America

We the People Cookies

Represent all of our nation's people at your bake sale! These sugar cookies can be tinted in different shades to make sure everyone feels included.

Ingredients

2¾ cups (14 oz/440 g) all-purpose flour, plus more for dusting

1 teaspoon baking powder

¼ teaspoon baking soda

¼ teaspoon salt

¾ cup (6 oz/185 g) plus 2 tablespoons unsalted butter, at room temperature

1 cup (7 oz/220 g) light brown sugar, firmly packed

1 large egg

1 tablespoon honey

1 tablespoon heavy cream

3 ounces (90 g) unsweetened chocolate, chopped, about ½ cup

Cookie Glaze

2¼ cups (9 oz/225 g) confectioners' sugar

2 tablespoons light corn syrup

1–2½ tablespoons milk

Specialty tools: Gingerbread people cookie cutters
Piping bag with plain round tip

★ In a bowl, whisk together the 2¾ cups flour, baking powder, baking soda, and salt. In a large bowl, using an electric mixer on medium-high speed, beat the butter and brown sugar until light and fluffy, 2–3 minutes. Add the egg and honey and beat on low speed until the egg is completely incorporated. Beating on low speed, slowly add the flour mixture and continue to beat until just incorporated, scraping down the sides of the bowl as needed. Add the cream and mix until incorporated. Divide the dough into 3 or 4 parts, depending upon how many different shades of cookie people you choose to make.

★ Place the chocolate in the top of a double boiler set over (not touching) simmering water. Heat, stirring often, until the chocolate is melted and smooth. Remove the bowl from over the water. Add warm chocolate, 1 tablespoon at a time, and work into each piece of dough until desired shade is achieved.

★ Press each piece of dough into a rough rectangle, wrap tightly in plastic wrap, and refrigerate until firm, at least 1 hour or up to overnight.

★ Make the Cookie Glaze: Sift the sugar into a bowl. Add the corn syrup and then add milk ½ tablespoon at a time until the glaze is a thick but pourable consistency. Stir until smooth, about 1 minute. Cover and store in the refrigerator for up to 3 days. Bring to room temperature or warm slightly before using.

★ Preheat the oven to 350°F (180°C). Line 3 baking sheets with parchment paper. On a lightly floured work surface, using a floured rolling pin, roll out the chilled dough until about ¼ inch (6 mm) thick. Using cookie cutters, cut the cookies into gingerbread people. Use a metal spatula to transfer the cookies to the prepared sheets, spacing them 1 inch (2.5 cm) apart. Press the dough scraps together, roll out, and cut out additional shapes.

★ Bake 1 sheet at a time until the cookies begin to turn a shade darker around the edges and are firm to the touch, 12–15 minutes. Let cool on the sheets for 5 minutes. Using the metal spatula, transfer to wire racks and let cool completely, about 30 minutes.

★ Once cookies are completely cool, decorate by piping with Cookie Glaze. Allow glaze to harden, at least 1 hour, before storing cookies in an airtight container, layered between parchment paper, at room temperature.

Makes about 24 cookies

Big Apple Oath-meal Cookies

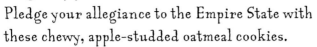

Pledge your allegiance to the Empire State with these chewy, apple-studded oatmeal cookies.

Ingredients

Vegetable oil cooking spray for greasing

½ cup (4 oz/125 g) plus 2 tablespoons unsalted butter, at room temperature

1 cup (7¾ oz/220 g) plus 2 tablespoons golden brown sugar, firmly packed

1 large egg

2 tablespoons whole milk

¾ teaspoon vanilla extract

1½ cups (4½ oz/135 g) old-fashioned rolled oats

1½ cups (7¼ oz/230 g) all-purpose flour

¾ teaspoon baking soda

¼ teaspoon salt

1 cup (4 oz/125 g) tart apple, peeled, cored, and chopped

1 cup (3 oz/90 g) dried apple, chopped

★ Preheat the oven to 350°F (180°C). Spray 2 cookie sheets with cooking spray.

★ In a large bowl, combine the butter and brown sugar. Using an electric mixer on high speed, beat until light and fluffy. Add the egg, milk, and vanilla and beat until very fluffy, about 2 minutes.

★ In a bowl, stir together the oats, flour, baking soda, and salt. Add the flour mixture to the butter mixture and mix on low speed until well blended. Add the fresh and dried apples and mix on low speed until combined.

★ Drop the dough by rounded tablespoonfuls onto the prepared cookie sheets, spacing the mounds about 2 inches (5 cm) apart. Bake until the cookies are golden brown, about 15 minutes. Transfer the cookies to wire racks to cool completely. Store in an airtight container in the refrigerator for up to 4 days.

Makes 24 cookies

★ Tip: To celebrate Michigan, the biggest cherry-producing state, try this variation: substitute the 1 cup chopped apple and 1 cup diced apple with ¾ cup dried cherries, ½ cup dark chocolate chips, and ½ cup walnuts.

Purple Mountain Majesties

Tinted purple and dusted with "snow," these sparkling macarons celebrate the splendor of the American landscape. Perfect for bake sales themed around environmental issues, this cookie serves as a delicious reminder that "America the beautiful" will only stay that way if we take good care of her.

Ingredients

1½ cups (6 oz/185 g) confectioners' sugar

1¼ cups (5 oz/140 g) blanched almond flour

3 large egg whites

Pinch salt

¼ cup (2 oz/60 g) granulated sugar

½ teaspoon vanilla or almond extract

Purple gel food coloring

White sanding sugar for sprinkling

Vanilla Creme Filling

¾ cup (6 oz/185 g) confectioners' sugar

1 cup (8 oz/250 g) unsalted butter, at room temperature

1½ teaspoons pure vanilla extract

Pinch salt

Specialty tools: Pastry bag with ½-inch (2.5-cm) round tip

★ Sift the confectioners' sugar into a large bowl. Whisk in the almond flour. In a clean, large bowl, using an electric mixer on medium-high speed, beat the egg whites until they form a dense foam, about 1 minute. Add the salt. Beating continuously, gradually add the granulated sugar. Beat until stiff, glossy peaks form, 3–4 minutes. Add the vanilla extract.

★ Add 1–2 drops of the food coloring to reach the desired color. Using a rubber spatula, gently fold the flour mixture into the beaten whites in 3 batches. Continue to fold just until the flour mixture is incorporated and the food coloring is evenly distributed. Be careful not to overmix, or the dough will deflate and become difficult to pipe.

★ Line 3 baking sheets with parchment paper. Spoon the dough into a large pastry bag with a ½-inch (12-mm) round tip. Pipe the dough onto the prepared sheets in 1½-inch (4-cm) circles, spacing them 1 inch (2.5 cm) apart. Sprinkle with sanding sugar. Let stand at room temperature, uncovered, for 1 hour.

★ Make the Vanilla Creme Filling: Sift the sugar into a large bowl and add the butter. Using an electric mixer on low speed, beat until combined. Increase the speed to medium-high and beat until light and fluffy, about 3 minutes. Add the vanilla and salt and beat on low speed just until combined. Store in the refrigerator for up to 3 days. Bring to room temperature before using.

★ Preheat the oven to 325°F (165°C). Bake the macarons until cookies feel firm to the touch but have not taken on any golden color, 12–15 minutes. Let cool completely on the baking sheets.

★ Turn half of the macarons bottom side up. Using a small offset spatula, spread 1 teaspoon of the filling over each macaron bottom. Gently press the remaining macarons, bottom side down, onto the filling. Refrigerate until firm, about 20 minutes. Store the cookies in an airtight container, layered between sheets of parchment paper, in the refrigerator for up to 2 days.

Makes about 35 cookies

Freedom Flags

Use colored batches of cookie dough to make old-fashioned sugar cookies look patriotic and colorful!

Ingredients

3 cups (15 oz/470 g) all-purpose flour, plus more for dusting

1 teaspoon baking powder

½ teaspoon salt

1 cup (8 oz/250 g) unsalted butter, at room temperature

1¼ cups (10 oz/315 g) sugar

1 large egg

2 teaspoons pure vanilla extract

1 tablespoon heavy cream

Red and blue gel food coloring

White sanding sugar

★ In a bowl, whisk together the 3 cups flour, baking powder, and salt. In a large bowl, using an electric mixer on medium-high speed, beat the butter and sugar until light and fluffy, 2–3 minutes. Add the egg and vanilla and beat on low speed until the egg is completely incorporated. Beating on low speed, slowly add the flour mixture and continue to beat until almost incorporated. Add the cream and beat on low speed until just incorporated, scraping down the sides of the bowl as needed.

★ Divide the dough into 3 equal parts. Add 1–2 drops of red gel food coloring to one-third of the dough and 1–2 drops of blue gel food coloring to another third. Knead each piece of colored dough separately until the color is completely incorporated. Keep one-third of the dough plain. Press the dough into a rough rectangle, wrap tightly in plastic wrap, and refrigerate until firm, at least 1 hour.

★ Once chilled, shape red dough into a rectangular log 8 inches (20 cm) long, 1½ inch (4 cm) wide, and ¾ inch (2 cm) thick. Shape blue dough and plain dough into logs of the same size. Stack the logs on top of one another and gently press them together to seal. Wrap tightly in plastic wrap and refrigerate until firm, about 1 hour.

★ Preheat the oven to 350°F (180°C). Line 3 baking sheets with parchment paper.

★ Using a chef's knife, trim the edges of the log to create a perfect rectangular shape. Brush the dough with water and roll in sanding sugar to coat. Cut the dough crosswise into slices ¼ inch (6 mm) thick. Using a metal spatula, transfer the slices to the prepared sheets, spacing them 1 inch (2.5 cm) apart.

★ Bake 1 batch at a time until the center of each cookie feels firm to the touch but has not yet taken on any golden color, 12–15 minutes. Let cool on the sheets for 5 minutes. Using a metal spatula, transfer to wire racks and let cool completely, about 30 minutes.

★ Store the cookies, layered between sheets of parchment paper, in an airtight container at room temperature for up to 3 days.

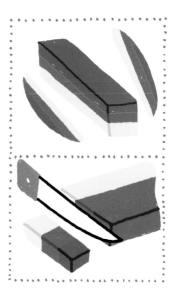

Makes about 30 cookies

★ Tip: You can easily adapt this recipe to make rainbow flags. Simply divide the dough into 6 equal parts and tint with red, orange, yellow, green, blue, and purple gel food coloring. Roll the logs following the instructions in the recipe, but make each 8 inches (20 cm) long, 2½ inches (6 cm) wide, and ¼ inch (6 mm) thick.

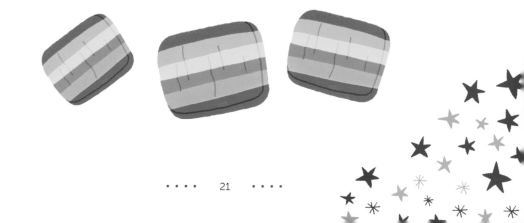

Born to Corn Sticks

Crunchy cornmeal sticks proudly represent America's heartland. They also remind us of America's first people, the Native Americans, who ate corn at every meal and introduced this valuable crop to the Pilgrims.

Ingredients

2¼ cups (11½ oz/360 g) all-purpose flour

3 tablespoons medium-grind yellow cornmeal, plus ¼ cup (1 oz/30 g)

½ teaspoon salt

1 cup (8 oz/250 g) unsalted butter, at room temperature

1 cup (4 oz/125 g) confectioners' sugar

½ cup (2 oz/30 g) walnuts, toasted and coarsely chopped

¼ cup (1½ oz/45 g) dried blueberries

½ cup (3 oz/90 g) dried cranberries

2 teaspoons finely grated lime zest

White sanding sugar for sprinkling

★ In a bowl, whisk together the flour, the 3 tablespoons cornmeal, and the salt. In a large bowl, using an electric mixer on medium-high speed, beat together the butter and confectioners' sugar until light and fluffy, 2–3 minutes. Beating on low speed, slowly add the flour mixture and continue to beat until almost incorporated, scraping down the sides of the bowl as needed. Add the walnuts, dried blueberries, dried cranberries, and lime zest and beat on low speed until just incorporated.

★ Form the dough into a log about 5 inches (13 cm) wide, 1¼ inches (3 cm) high, and 7 inches (18 cm) long. Sprinkle the ¼ cup cornmeal onto the log, using your hands to gently press it into the dough. Wrap the log tightly in plastic wrap and refrigerate for at least 1 hour or up to overnight.

★ Preheat the oven to 350°F (180°C). Line 3 baking sheets with parchment paper.

★ Use a chef's knife to cut the log crosswise into slices ¼ inch (6 mm) thick. Transfer the cookies to the prepared sheets, spacing them 1 inch (2.5 cm) apart. Sprinkle with the sanding sugar.

★ Bake until the edges turn light golden brown but the centers are barely colored, 16–18 minutes. Let cool on the sheets for 5 minutes. Using a metal spatula, transfer the cookies to wire racks and let cool completely, about 30 minutes. Store the cookies in an airtight container, layered between sheets of parchment paper, at room temperature for up to 4 days.

Makes about 25 cookies

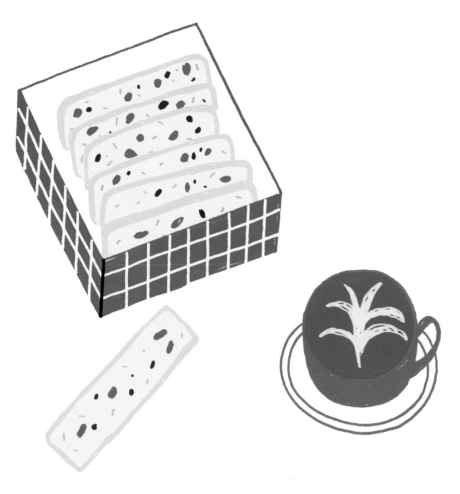

Eagle Rights for All

Marshmallows dipped in melted chocolate and decorated with coconut "feathers" offer a sweet tribute to America's national bird.

Ingredients

2¼ cups (11½ oz/360 g) all-purpose flour, plus more for dusting

⅓ cup (1 oz/30 g) unsweetened cocoa powder

½ teaspoon baking powder

½ teaspoon baking soda

¼ teaspoon salt

¾ cup (6 oz/185 g) unsalted butter, at room temperature

1 cup (7 oz/220 g) light brown sugar, firmly packed

¼ cup (2 oz/60 g) granulated sugar

1 large egg

1 teaspoon pure vanilla extract

2 cups (12 oz/360 g) white chocolate chips

2 cups (12 oz/360 g) dark chocolate chips, plus additional for decorating

30 large marshmallows

1 cup (7 oz/220 g) shredded sweetened coconut

30 almond slivers

★ In a bowl, whisk together the 2¼ cups flour, cocoa powder, baking powder, baking soda, and salt. In a large bowl, using an electric mixer on medium-high speed, beat the butter, brown sugar, and granulated sugar until light and fluffy, 2–3 minutes. Add the egg and vanilla and beat on low speed until the egg is completely incorporated. Beating on low speed, slowly add the flour mixture and continue to beat until just incorporated, scraping down the sides of the bowl as needed.

★ Press the dough into a roughly 2-inch (5-cm) wide log, wrap tightly in plastic wrap, and refrigerate until firm, at least 1 hour or up to overnight. (The dough can be wrapped well and frozen for up to 1 month.)

★ Preheat the oven to 350°F (180°C). Line 3 baking sheets with parchment paper. On a lightly floured work surface, using a knife, cut the cookies into ½-inch (12-mm) thick rounds. Transfer the cookies to the prepared sheets, spacing them 1 inch (2.5 cm) apart.

★ Bake 1 sheet at a time until the cookies are firm to the touch, 12—15 minutes. Let cool on the sheets for 5 minutes. Using a metal spatula, transfer to wire racks and let cool completely, about 30 minutes.

★ While cookies are cooling, create the marshmallow eagle heads. Melt white chocolate and dark chocolate chips in separate double boilers or in metal bowls set over (but not touching) simmering water in a pot. Dip marshmallows three-quarters of the way into the white chocolate, and then roll in coconut flakes to coat. Dip the bottom quarter of the marshmallow in the melted dark chocolate, and set on chocolate cookie, pressing lightly to fuse marshmallow and cookie together. Allow the chocolate to partially set, about 10 minutes, then use a skewer or a toothpick to poke 2 small "eye" holes into the marshmallow. Insert 2 chocolate chips to make eyes. Beneath the eyes, make a small slit using a sharp knife and insert an almond sliver beak to make a charming eagle face!

Makes 30 cookies

Jammin' for Justice Cookies

Swirl sweet strawberry jam into crisp cookies and give a nod to the state fruit of Louisiana—home to the tallest state capitol building in the U.S.A.

Ingredients

3 cups (15 oz/470 g) all-purpose flour, plus more for dusting

1 teaspoon baking powder

½ teaspoon salt

1 cup (8 oz/250 g) unsalted butter, at room temperature

1¼ cups (10 oz/315 g) sugar

1 large egg

2 teaspoons pure vanilla extract

1 tablespoon heavy cream

2 cups (20 oz/625 g) strawberry jam

¼ cup (2 oz/60 g) sanding sugar or granulated sugar

★ Preheat the oven to 350°F (180°C). Line 3 baking sheets with parchment paper.

★ In a bowl, whisk together the 3 cups flour, baking powder, and salt. In a large bowl, using an electric mixer on medium-high speed, beat the butter and sugar until light and fluffy, 2–3 minutes. Add the egg and vanilla and beat on low speed until the egg is completely incorporated. Beating on low speed, slowly add the flour mixture and continue to beat until almost incorporated. Add the cream and beat on low speed until just incorporated, scraping down the sides of the bowl as needed.

★ On a lightly floured work surface, using a floured rolling pin, roll the dough into a 16-by-12-inch (40-by-30cm) rectangle about ¼ inch (6 mm) thick. Starting at the short end closest to you and using an offset spatula, evenly spread 1 cup (10 oz/310 g) of the jam over half of the dough, leaving a ½-inch (12-mm) border. Starting at the end covered in jam, roll up the dough tightly until you reach the center point of the dough, forming a log.

★ Carefully invert the dough, flipping the log so that the long portion of dough not covered in jam is on your right and the rolled log is now on your left. Evenly spread the remaining 1 cup of jam onto the other half of the dough. Roll up the dough, tightly forming a log, until you reach the center of the dough. The two rolls should be rolled up in opposite directions, meeting in the center. Gently press the two rolls together. Use a chef's knife to trim the uneven ends. Refrigerate or freeze the log until firm, about 10 minutes.

★ Using a sharp knife, cut the roll crosswise into 30 slices about ½ inch thick. Use a metal spatula to transfer the slices to the prepared sheets, spacing them 1½ inches (4 cm) apart. Sprinkle each cookie with sugar.

★ Bake the cookies until the edges are lightly golden and the tops are barely colored, 16–19 minutes. Let cool completely, about 30 minutes. Store the cookies in an airtight container, layered between sheets of parchment paper, at room temperature for up to 4 days.

Makes about 30 cookies

Fourth of July Pinwheels

These festive pinwheel cookies feature blackberry jam heart centers, in a nod to the state fruit of Alabama—whose state motto is "We dare defend our rights."

Ingredients

2 large eggs, 1 with white separated and yolk reserved for another use

3 cups (15 oz/470 g) all-purpose flour, plus more for dusting

1 teaspoon baking powder

½ teaspoon salt

1 cup (8 oz/250 g) unsalted butter, at room temperature

1¼ cups (10 oz/315 g) sugar

2 teaspoons pure vanilla extract

1 tablespoon heavy cream

White sanding sugar for sprinkling

1¼ cups (15 oz/420 g) blackberry jam or preserves

★ Preheat the oven to 350°F (180°C). Line 3 baking sheets with parchment paper.

★ In a small bowl, whisk together the egg white from 1 egg and 2 teaspoons water, and set aside.

★ In a bowl, whisk together the 3 cups flour, baking powder, and salt. In a large bowl, using an electric mixer on medium-high speed, beat the butter and sugar until light and fluffy, 2–3 minutes. Add the whole egg and vanilla and beat on low speed until the egg is completely incorporated. Beating on low speed, slowly add the flour mixture and continue to beat until almost incorporated. Add the cream and beat on low speed until just incorporated, scraping down the sides of the bowl as needed.

★ On a lightly floured work surface, using a floured rolling pin, roll the dough into an 11-by-16-inch (28-by-40cm) rectangle about ¼ inch (6 mm) thick. Using a ruler as a straightedge and a pizza wheel or paring knife, trim the edges of the dough to form a 10-by-15-inch (25-by-38-cm) rectangle. Then cut the dough into twenty-four 2½-inch (6-cm) squares.

★ Use a metal spatula to transfer the cookies to the prepared sheets, spacing them 1 inch (2.5 cm) apart. Using the pizza wheel or a sharp paring knife, make diagonal cuts from each corner three-fourths of the way toward the center of each square. Each corner should have 2 points. Fold every other point toward the center, gently pressing it down to seal. Lightly brush the cookies with the egg white mixture. Sprinkle with sanding sugar. Spoon 1 tablespoon of the jam into the center of each cookie.

★ Bake until the cookies are lightly golden brown around the edges and just barely golden near the center, 16–19 minutes. Let cool on the sheets for 5 minutes. Using a metal spatula, transfer to wire racks and let cool completely, about 30 minutes. Store the cookies, layered between sheets of parchment paper, in an airtight container at room temperature for up to 3 days.

Makes 24 cookies

Orange You Glad You're American! Cookies

These orange truffle cookies, topped with zesty orange peel, pay homage to the Sunshine State.

Ingredients

½ cup (2½ oz/75 g) all-purpose flour, plus more for dusting

¼ cup (¾ oz/20 g) unsweetened cocoa powder

¼ teaspoon baking soda

¼ teaspoon salt

8 ounces (250 g) bittersweet chocolate, coarsely chopped

6 tablespoons (3 oz/90 g) unsalted butter, cut into pieces

2 large eggs, at room temperature

¾ cup (6 oz/185 g) sugar

1 teaspoon orange extract

Zest of 2 oranges

¼ cup (1¾ oz/50 g) coarse sugar

Dark Chocolate Cream

¾ cup (6 oz/185 g) confectioners' sugar

1 cup (8 oz/250 g) unsalted butter, at room temperature

1½ teaspoons pure vanilla extract

Pinch salt

3 ounces (90 g) unsweetened chocolate

Specialty tools: Pastry bag with a ½-inch (12-mm) rose petal tip

★ In a bowl, whisk together the ½ cup flour, cocoa, baking soda, and salt. Place about three-fourths of the chocolate and all of the butter in a heatproof bowl set over (but not touching) barely simmering water. Heat, stirring frequently, until the chocolate is completely melted and smooth, 4–5 minutes. Remove the bowl from the heat and let cool to lukewarm, about 15 minutes.

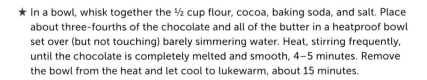

★ In a large bowl, using an electric mixer on medium-high speed, beat together the eggs and sugar until pale and thick, about 2 minutes. Add the orange extract and beat to combine. Add the melted chocolate and, using a rubber spatula, gently stir to combine. Using the spatula, gently stir in the flour mixture in 2 batches just until incorporated. Add the remaining chopped chocolate and stir just until incorporated. Cover and refrigerate the dough until well chilled, at least 1 hour or up to overnight.

★ Make the Dark Chocolate Cream: Sift the sugar into a large bowl and add the butter. Using an electric mixer on low speed, beat until combined. Increase the speed to medium-high and beat until light and fluffy, about 3 minutes. Add the vanilla and salt, and beat on low speed just until combined. In a heat-proof bowl set over (but not touching) simmering water, heat the unsweetened chocolate, stirring frequently, until completely melted, about 4 minutes; set aside to cool completely. Add the chocolate to the beaten butter and sugar mixture and beat on low speed until just combined. Refrigerate until firm, about 30 minutes.

★ Preheat the oven to 350°F (180°C). Line 3 baking sheets with parchment paper.

★ Scoop up rounded teaspoonfuls of the cookie dough and, using floured hands, roll into balls. Place on the prepared sheets, spaced about 1 inch (2.5 cm) apart. Bake until the cookies feel firm in the center but have not yet taken on additional color, 10–12 minutes. Let cool on the sheets for 5 minutes. Using a metal spatula, transfer the cookies to wire racks to cool completely, about 30 minutes.

★ Spoon the Dark Chocolate Cream into a pastry bag fitted with a ½-inch (12-mm) rose petal tip. Pipe 2 rows of filling in a zigzag pattern down the center of each cookie. Zest the oranges using a microplane or zester. Sprinkle cookies with orange zest and coarse sugar just before serving. Store the cookies in a single layer in an airtight container at room temperature for up to 3 days.

Makes about 40 cookies

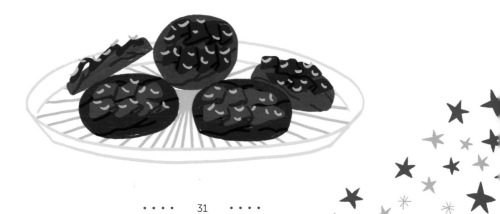

Stripey Star Bars

Pecan streusel bars give a maple-flavored nod to New England. Cut into star shapes and striped with glaze, these cookies are star-spangled winners.

Ingredients

2½ cups (12½ oz/390 g) all-purpose flour

1 teaspoon ground cinnamon

½ teaspoon salt

1½ cups (6 oz/185 g) pecans, finely chopped

1 cup (8 oz/250 g) unsalted butter, at room temperature.

½ cup (3½ oz/105 g) light brown sugar, firmly packed

½ cup (2 oz/60 g) confectioners' sugar

2 teaspoons maple extract

Vanilla Glaze

1 cup (4 oz/125 g) confectioners' sugar

4 teaspoons milk

1 teaspoon pure vanilla extract

Red and blue food coloring (optional)

Specialty tools: Star-shaped cookie cutters (optional)

★ Preheat the oven to 350°F (180°C). Butter a 9-by-13-inch (23-by-33-cm) baking pan. Line with parchment paper, leaving at least a 1-inch (2.5-cm) overhang on the long sides.

★ In a large bowl, whisk together the flour, cinnamon, salt, and pecans. In a separate large bowl, using an electric mixer on medium-high speed, beat together the 1 cup butter, the brown sugar, and the confectioners' sugar until light and fluffy, about 2 minutes. Beating on low speed, add the flour mixture and maple extract and continue to beat just until incorporated. The mixture should resemble coarse crumbs.

★ Transfer 3 cups of the dough to the prepared pan. Cover with a sheet of parchment paper. Using the bottom of a measuring cup, press the dough evenly into the pan, lifting the parchment occasionally to make sure that it doesn't stick. The dough should be firmly packed, without holes or cracks. Remove parchment and cover evenly with the remaining dough, sprinkling it over the top and squeezing some of the dough to form large clumps.

★ Bake until lightly golden, 16–18 minutes. Transfer the pan to a wire rack and let cool completely, about 1 hour.

★ Make the Vanilla Glaze: Sift the sugar into a bowl. Add the milk and vanilla and stir until completely smooth, about 1 minute. If you wish to make red, white, and blue stripes, divide the glaze into thirds. Add 5–7 drops of red food coloring to one-third, stirring to combine, and 5–7 drops of blue to another third, until desired color is reached. Cover and store in the refrigerator for up to 3 days. Bring to room temperature or warm slightly before using.

★ After bars are completely cool, run a metal spatula around the edges of the pan. Grasping parchment on either end, lift bars carefully out of the pan. Cut into squares or into star shapes using cookie cutter. Drizzle with the glaze and let set for at least 10 minutes. Store the bars in an airtight container, layered between sheets of parchment paper, at room temperature for up to 3 days.

Makes about 18 bar cookies

★ Tip: If you cut your bars into star shapes, you will have leftover crumbles that make a perfect topping for ice cream!

CHAPTER 2

Cupcake Country

March-mallow Creme Cupcakes

These velvety chocolate cupcakes topped with pink
marshmallow creme will look especially sweet
when lined up in rows as if marching.

Ingredients

¼ cup (¾ oz/20 g) natural cocoa powder

3 tablespoons plus 1½ teaspoons boiling water

⅓ cup (2½ fl oz/75 ml) buttermilk

1¼ cup (5 oz/150 g) all-purpose flour

½ teaspoon baking soda

⅛ teaspoon kosher salt

¼ cup (2 oz/60g) unsalted butter, at room temperature

⅓ cup (½ oz/70 g) granulated sugar

2 tablespoons plus 2 teaspoons light brown sugar, firmly packed

1 large egg

½ teaspoon pure vanilla extract

Marshmallow Creme Frosting

6 tablespoons confectioners' sugar

1½ tablespoons unsalted butter, at room temperature

¼ cup (2 oz/62 g) purchased marshmallow creme

¼ teaspoon pure vanilla extract

1½ teaspoons heavy cream

Red food coloring

Specialty tools: Pastry bag with star tip (optional)

★ Preheat oven to 350°F (180°C). Line 6 standard muffin cups with liners—for extra
pizzazz, use liners in a pattern themed to your event!

★ In a bowl, whisk the cocoa powder into the boiling water. Let cool to lukewarm, then whisk in the buttermilk. In another bowl, sift together the flour, baking soda, and salt.

★ In the bowl of a mixer fitted with the paddle attachment, beat the butter and sugar on medium speed until combined. Add the egg and beat well. Add the vanilla. Reduce the speed to low and add the dry ingredients in 3 additions alternately with the cocoa-buttermilk mixture in 2 additions, starting and ending with the dry ingredients. Beat just until combined.

★ Divide among the prepared muffin cups, filling them nearly full. Bake until the cupcakes are puffed and slightly springy to the touch, and a toothpick inserted into the center of a cupcake comes out clean, about 20 minutes. Let cool slightly, then remove the cupcakes from the pan and cool completely on wire racks.

★ Make the Marshmallow Creme Frosting: in the bowl of a mixer, sift the sugar over the butter. Fit the mixer with the paddle attachment and beat on medium speed until lightened. Add the marshmallow creme, vanilla extract, and cream and beat until light and fluffy. Add 2–3 drops red food coloring, until desired shade of pink is reached, and fold in until incorporated.

★ Once cupcakes are completely cool, spread with Marshmallow Creme Frosting—or pipe frosting using a pastry bag fitted with a star tip for a more decorative look. The frosted cupcakes can be refrigerated in an airtight container for up to 4 days; bring to room temperature before serving.

Makes 6 cupcakes

U.S. Mints

Rich chocolate-mint cupcakes topped with crushed peppermints will have your guests saying, "Show me the money!"

Ingredients

¾ cup (3 oz/90 g) semisweet chocolate chips

6 tablespoons (3 oz/90 g) unsalted butter

½ teaspoon peppermint extract

½ cup (2 oz/60 g) cake flour

2 tablespoons unsweetened cocoa powder

2 eggs, separated

½ cup (4 oz/125 g) sugar

⅛ teaspoon salt

Green and white-striped peppermints, crushed

White Chocolate Mint Icing

2 ounces (60 g) white chocolate, chopped

1 tablespoon heavy cream

½ teaspoon peppermint extract

Green gel food coloring

★ Preheat the oven to 350°F (180°C). Prepare a 6-cup standard muffin pan by greasing or inserting liners.

★ In a small saucepan over very low heat, melt the chocolate and butter. Stir in the peppermint extract and set aside. In a medium bowl, whisk together the flour and cocoa. In another bowl, with an electric mixer on medium speed, beat the egg yolks and half of the sugar until pale. Stir in the chocolate and butter mixture.

★ In a bowl, beat the egg whites and salt to soft peaks. Beat in the remaining sugar until stiff peaks form. Stir the flour mixture into the chocolate mixture. With a rubber spatula, fold in the egg whites in three batches.

★ Divide the batter among the prepared cups. Bake 20–25 minutes. Cool on a wire rack for 10 minutes, then turn out and cool completely.

★ Make the White Chocolate Mint Icing: In a double boiler (or in a metal bowl set atop a pot of simmering water on the stove), melt the white chocolate and cream together. Stir in the peppermint extract. Remove from heat and stir in the food coloring. Cool to room temperature.

★ Ice the cupcakes once the cupcakes and icing have cooled. Top with the crushed peppermints.

Makes 6 cupcakes

Berry Proud to Be American Cupcakes

These luscious cupcakes brim with raspberries, blueberries ... and pride.

Ingredients

⅔ cup (4 oz/120 g) all-purpose flour

1½ teaspoons baking powder

¼ teaspoon ground cinnamon

Pinch baking soda

1 tablespoon plus 2 teaspoons light brown sugar, firmly packed

3 tablespoons cream cheese

1 egg, lightly beaten

¼ cup (2 fl oz/60 ml) milk

1½ tablespoons unsalted butter, melted

¼ teaspoon vanilla extract

¼ cup (1 oz/30 g) raspberries

¼ cup (1¼ oz/38 g) blueberries

Confectioners' sugar, for dusting

★ Preheat the oven to 350°F (180°C). Prepare a 6-cup standard muffin pan by greasing or inserting liners.

★ In a mixing bowl, whisk together the flour, baking powder, cinnamon, and baking soda. Stir in the brown sugar. Using a pastry blender or two butter knives held criss-crossed, cut in the cream cheese until the mixture resembles pea-sized crumbs.

★ In a small bowl, combine the egg, milk, melted butter, and vanilla extract. Add all at once to the flour mixture and stir just until moistened. Fold in the berries. Divide the mixture evenly among the prepared cups.

★ Bake until the tops spring back when tapped lightly, 20–25 minutes. Cool in the pan on a wire rack for 10 minutes, then turn out and cool completely. Before serving, dust lightly with confectioners' sugar.

Makes 6 cupcakes

Have a Heart Cupcakes

Each coconut-raspberry cupcake is filled with a heart
of jam and topped with a strawberry kiss.

Ingredients

1 egg

1 tablespoon plus 1 teaspoon granulated sugar

¼ cup (1½ oz/45 g) all-purpose flour

¼ teaspoon baking powder

2 tablespoons flaked coconut

1 tablespoon unsalted butter, melted

2 tablespoons raspberry jam

2–3 large strawberries

Confectioners' sugar, for dusting

★ In a mixing bowl, using a hand-held electric mixer on medium-high speed,
beat the egg and sugar until the mixture is thick and pale and forms a ribbon
when the beaters are lifted out. In a separate bowl, whisk together the flour and
baking powder. With a rubber spatula, fold about half of the flour mixture into
the egg mixture; then fold in half of the coconut. Repeat with the remainder
of each. Fold in the melted butter. Cover the bowl and chill in the refrigerator
for 25 minutes.

★ Meanwhile, preheat the oven to 400°F (200°C). Prepare a 6-cup standard muffin
pan by greasing or inserting liners.

★ Distribute half of the batter evenly among the prepared cups. Spoon 1 scant
teaspoon of jam into the center of each cup. Cover with the remaining batter.
Bake until the tops spring back when tapped lightly, 15–20 minutes. Turn out
onto wire racks to cool completely.

★ Remove stems from strawberries by cutting a circle around the stem and
lifting gently. Slice the strawberries. Before serving, dust the cupcakes with
confectioners' sugar, and top each with a sliced strawberry "heart."

Makes 6 cupcakes

★ Tip: Instead of raspberry jam, fill these cupcakes with your favorite flavor—cherry, blueberry, orange marmalade, or even lemon curd.

Better Together Cupcakes

Black and white cupcakes come together to form a deliciously perfect union.

Ingredients

½ cup (4 oz/125 g) sugar

½ cup (4 fl oz/125 ml) sour cream

⅓ cup (3 fl oz/80 ml) vegetable oil

1 egg

½ teaspoon vanilla extract

¾ cup (3 oz/90 g) cake flour

⅓ cup (1 oz/30 g) unsweetened cocoa powder

¾ teaspoon baking soda

Chocolate Icing

2 tablespoons heavy cream

2 teaspoons light corn syrup

⅓ cup (1⅔ oz/50 g) semisweet mini chocolate chips

White Icing

½ cup (2 oz/60 g) confectioners' sugar

¼ teaspoon vanilla extract

1–2 tablespoons heavy cream

★ Preheat the oven to 350°F (180°C). Prepare a 6-cup standard muffin pan by greasing or inserting liners.

★ In a medium bowl, whisk together the sugar, sour cream, oil, egg, and vanilla. Sift in the flour, cocoa, and baking soda. Stir until blended. Divide the batter equally among the prepared cups.

★ Bake until the tops spring back when tapped lightly, 20–25 minutes. Cool on a wire rack for 10 minutes, then turn out to cool completely.

★ Make the Chocolate Icing: Combine the cream and corn syrup in a small, heavy saucepan and bring to a simmer over medium-low heat. Remove from the heat and stir in the chocolate chips until smooth. Let cool until it reaches a thick but fluid spreading consistency.

★ Make the White Icing: In a small bowl, stir together the sugar, vanilla extract, and enough of the cream to form a smooth icing.

★ Spread each icing over half of the top of each cupcake. Let stand until set, about 1 hour.

Makes 6 cupcakes

Three Cheers for America! Cupcakes

Say hooray for the U.S. of A.—times three—with these crowd-pleasing triple chocolate cupcakes.

Ingredients

1 cup (5 oz/155 g) self-rising flour

¼ teaspoon baking soda

3 tablespoons unsweetened cocoa powder

¼ cup (2 oz/60 g) sugar

¼ cup (1½ oz/50 g) white chocolate chips

¼ cup (3 oz/90 g) semisweet chocolate chips

¼ cup milk chocolate chips

1 egg, lightly beaten

¾ cup (6 fl oz/180 ml) plus 1 tablespoon milk

2 tablespoons unsalted butter, melted

Red, white, and blue star candy confetti (optional)

★ Preheat the oven to 350°F (180°C). Prepare a 6-cup standard muffin pan by greasing or inserting liners.

★ In a mixing bowl, whisk together the flour, baking soda, and cocoa. Stir in the sugar, the white chocolate chips, and the semisweet chips. In a small bowl, mix the egg, ¾ cup of the milk, and the butter. Add all at once to the flour mixture and stir until just moistened.

★ Divide the batter evenly among the prepared cups. Bake until the tops spring back when lightly touched, 20–25 minutes. Cool in the pan for 5 minutes, then turn out onto a wire rack to cool completely.

★ Meanwhile, put the milk chocolate chips and a tablespoon of milk in a microwave-safe bowl and melt in short bursts in the microwave. Stir until smooth. Using a teaspoon, swirl the melted chocolate thickly over the top of each cupcake. Sprinkle with red, white, and blue candy stars.

Makes 6 cupcakes

★ Tip: Top each cupcake with an American flag toothpick to boost the celebration!

Peel Away the Partisanship Cupcakes

Sweet and tart unite as one in these satisfying coconut cakes topped with twists of lemon peel.

Ingredients

5 tablespoons (2½ oz/75 g) unsalted butter

1 cup (5 oz/155 g) self-rising flour

⅔ cup (2⅔ oz/80 g) grated dried coconut

⅓ cup (3 oz/90 g) sugar

1 egg, lightly beaten

½ cup (4 fl oz/125 ml) milk

1 teaspoon grated lemon zest

2 tablespoons lemon juice

¼ cup (1½ oz/45 g) all-purpose flour

⅔ cup (2⅔ oz/80 g) sweetened shredded coconut

Vanilla Buttercream

1½ cups (6 oz/190 g) confectioners' sugar

½ cup (4 oz/120 g) unsalted butter, at room temperature

½ teaspoon vanilla extract

1–2 tablespoons heavy cream

★ Preheat the oven to 350°F (180°C). Prepare a 6-cup standard muffin pan by greasing or inserting liners. Melt 1½ tablespoons of the butter; put the remainder in the refrigerator to chill.

★ In a large mixing bowl, sift the self-rising flour. Stir in ½ cup (2 oz/60 g) of the grated dried coconut and ¼ cup (2 oz/60 g) of the sugar. Make a well in the center. In a small bowl, combine the egg, milk, melted butter, and lemon juice. Add all at once to the flour mixture and stir just until moistened. Divide evenly among the prepared cups.

★ Put the all-purpose flour and remaining grated coconut and sugar in a small bowl. Cut the chilled butter into cubes and rub it into the dry ingredients with your fingertips until the mixture resembles coarse crumbs. Spoon evenly over the cupcakes.

★ Bake until the tops are springy when tapped lightly, 20–25 minutes. Cool in the pan for 5 minutes, then turn out to cool completely.

★ Make the Vanilla Buttercream: In a medium bowl, use a hand-held electric mixer on medium speed to beat together the confectioners' sugar and butter until blended. Beat in the vanilla, then beat in enough of the cream to achieve a soft consistency suitable for spreading.

★ Spread the Vanilla Buttercream on top of the cooled cupcakes and sprinkle evenly with the shredded coconut, pressing it gently into the buttercream. Sprinkle lemon zest on top.

Makes 6 cupcakes

Care-it Cakes

Show family and friends you care with these double-decker carrot cupcakes topped with a heart-shaped dollop of frosting.

Ingredients

1 cup (5 oz/155 g) all-purpose flour

1 teaspoon baking powder

¼ teaspoon salt

1 teaspoon ground cinnamon

¼ teaspoon grated nutmeg

2 eggs

½ cup (3½ oz/105 g) light brown sugar, firmly packed.

½ cup (4 oz/125 g) granulated sugar

½ cup (4 fl oz/125 ml) vegetable oil

1½ cups (7 oz/215 g) grated carrot

½ cup (3 oz/90 g) raisins

Cream Cheese Frosting

¼ cup (2 oz/60 g) unsalted butter, at room temperature

4 ounces (125 g) cream cheese, at room temperature

1 cup (4 oz/125 g) confectioners' sugar

½ teaspoon vanilla extract

Specialty tools: Pastry bag and decorating tip or heart-shaped cookie cutter (optional)

★ Preheat the oven to 350°F (180°C). Prepare a 6-cup standard muffin pan by greasing or inserting liners.

★ In a medium mixing bowl, whisk together the flour, baking powder, salt, cinnamon, and nutmeg. In a separate bowl, using a hand-held electric mixer on medium speed, beat together the eggs, brown sugar, granulated sugar, and oil. Stir into the dry ingredients just until blended. Stir in the carrot and raisins.

★ Divide the batter equally among the prepared muffin cups. Bake until the tops spring back when tapped lightly, 20–25 minutes. Cool on a wire rack for 5 minutes, then turn out the cupcakes and cool completely.

★ Make the Cream Cheese Frosting: In a mixing bowl, use a hand-held mixer on medium speed to beat together the butter, cream cheese, sugar, and vanilla until smooth.

★ With a serrated knife, cut each cupcake in half horizontally. Spread some of the Cream Cheese Frosting over the cut surface of the bottom halves. Replace the top halves, and add a dollop to the tops—you can pipe the shape of a heart using a pastry bag or use a cookie cutter as a "stencil" and fill with frosting.

Makes 6 cupcakes

Pride, Bravery, and Justice Cupcakes

Moist banana cupcakes provide the perfect platform for America's favorite sandwich-turned-frosting—peanut butter and jelly.

Ingredients

1 cup (4 oz/125 g) cake flour

1 teaspoon baking powder

¼ teaspoon salt

½ cup (4 oz/125 g) sugar

¼ cup (2½ oz/80 g) creamy peanut butter

1 egg

½ cup (4 oz/125 g) mashed ripe banana (1 small banana)

¼ cup (2½ oz/75 g) strawberry jam

Peanut Butter Frosting

¾ cup (7½ oz/235 g) creamy peanut butter

½ cup (2½ oz/75 g) confectioners' sugar

1–2 tablespoons heavy cream

★ Preheat the oven to 350°F (180°C). Prepare a 6-cup standard muffin pan by greasing or inserting liners.

★ In a small bowl, whisk together the flour, baking powder, and salt. In a medium bowl, using a handheld mixer on medium speed, beat together the sugar and peanut butter until light. Beat in the egg, then the mashed banana. Gradually beat in the dry ingredients just until combined. Divide the batter equally among the prepared cups.

★ Bake until the tops spring back when tapped lightly, 20–25 minutes. Cool on a wire rack for 5 minutes, then turn out and cool completely.

★ Make the Peanut Butter Frosting: Place the peanut butter in a small bowl and use a hand-held mixer on medium speed to beat until fluffy. Gradually beat in the sugar. Beat in enough of the cream to reach a spreading consistency.

★ Spread the frosting on the cooled cupcakes. Make a shallow well in frosting at the center of the cupcake and fill with a dollop of strawberry jam. Swirl jam into the peanut butter frosting for extra effect!

Makes 6 cupcakes

We Can—with Pecan! Coffee Cupcakes

Yes, we can make the world a sweeter place!

Ingredients

½ cup (4 oz/125 g) granulated sugar

½ cup (4 oz/125 g) butter, chopped into small pieces

¾ teaspoon vanilla extract

2 eggs

1⅓ cups (7 oz/215 g) self-rising flour, sifted

¼ teaspoon baking soda

¾ cup (6 oz/172 g) sour cream

⅔ cup (2⅔ oz/80 g) chopped pecans

½ teaspoon ground cinnamon

1 tablespoon plus 1 teaspoon firmly packed brown sugar

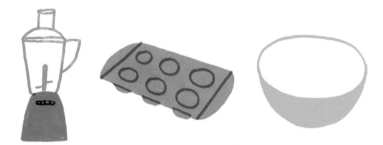

★ Preheat the oven to 350°F (180°C). Prepare a 6-cup standard muffin pan by greasing or inserting liners.

★ In a food processor with a stainless-steel blade, combine the granulated sugar, butter, vanilla, eggs, flour, baking soda, and sour cream. Process until smooth, 1–2 minutes. Distribute half of the batter evenly among the cups of the prepared muffin pan.

★ In a small bowl, combine the pecans, cinnamon, and brown sugar. Sprinkle half over the batter in the pan. Top with the remaining batter, then sprinkle with the remaining pecan mixture.

★ Bake until the cupcakes spring back when lightly touched, 20–25 minutes. Cool in the pan for 5 minutes. Serve warm, or transfer to a wire rack to cool.

Makes 6 cupcakes

★ Tip: For a fun flavor variation—or to accommodate people who can't eat nuts—swap in chopped dried cherries, cranberries, or apricots for the pecans.

CHAPTER 3

Sweet Land of Liberty

Freedom Fudge

Feel free to dig in to these scrumptious, candy-topped fudge squares.

Ingredients

½ cup (4 oz/125 g) unsalted butter, melted, plus more to grease pan

2 cups (1 lb/500 g) granulated sugar

2 cups (14 oz/440 g) light brown sugar, firmly packed

½ cup (5 oz/155 g) light corn syrup

1 cup (8 fl oz/250 ml) half-and-half

¼ teaspoon kosher salt

½ pound (250 g) bittersweet or semisweet chocolate, coarsely chopped

2 cups (3½ oz/105 g) red, white, and blue candy-coated chocolates

Specialty tools: Pastry brush
Candy thermometer

★ Lightly butter a 9-by-11-inch (23-by-28-cm) or 9-by-13-inch (23-by-33-cm) baking pan.

★ In a large, heavy saucepan, bring the butter, granulated sugar, brown sugar, corn syrup, half-and-half, and salt to a boil over medium heat, stirring constantly. Using a pastry brush dipped in hot water, brush down any sugar crystals that form on the sides of the pan. Boil for 2½ minutes and then add the chocolate and stir until melted and well blended. Continue to boil, without stirring, until a candy thermometer clipped to the side of the pan reads 234°F (112°C), 7–10 minutes.

★ Remove from the heat and let cool until almost room temperature, or 110°F (43°C) on the thermometer, about 15 minutes. Using an electric mixer, beat the fudge until the color dulls and the fudge is creamy, 2–3 minutes.

★ Spoon half the fudge into the prepared pan and sprinkle half the candies over it. Top with the remaining fudge and smooth surface with a spatula. Sprinkle with the remaining candies, pressing the candy and fudge together with the spatula. Cover the pan with foil and refrigerate until firm, about 6 hours. Cut into squares and serve.

Makes about 32 squares

Rights Crispies Treats ✦

Treat yourself to crisped rice stars drizzled with white chocolate and showered with celebratory rainbow sprinkles.

Ingredients

5 tablespoons (2½ oz/70 g) butter, plus extra to grease tools

4 cups (8 oz/225 g) mini-size marshmallows

½ cup (2 oz/60 g) vanilla cake mix

5 cups (4½ oz/125 g) crisped rice cereal

3 tablespoons rainbow jimmies, plus extra for decorating

4 ounces (125 g) white chocolate, finely chopped

12 lollipop sticks

Specialty tools: Star-shaped cookie cutters (optional)

★ Line a 9-by-13 inch (23-by-33-cm) baking pan with wax paper.

★ In a large saucepan, melt butter over low heat. Stir in marshmallows, continuing to stir until melted. Remove from heat. Add cake mix and stir until smooth. Add the crisped rice cereal and stir until completely coated. Add the 3 tablespoons of jimmies and stir until well distributed.

★ Press the mixture into prepared pan, using the back of a buttered spoon to make the surface as level as possible. Allow to cool, about 20 minutes.

★ Use a buttered cookie cutter to cut star shapes from the treats. Form leftover pieces into squares and cut additional treats. (If you prefer, you can simply cut the treats into squares.)

★ Place the chocolate in the top of a double boiler or in a heatproof bowl. Place over (not touching) barely simmering water and heat, stirring occasionally, until melted and smooth.

★ Dip lollipop sticks into chocolate and insert into treats. Drizzle treats with the melted chocolate and sprinkle with additional jimmies. Allow chocolate to harden about 10 minutes before serving.

Makes about 12 treats

★ Tip: In place of the multicolored jimmies, substitute candies in the colors of the rainbow!

Whoopie! We're American! Pies

Miniature chocolate cookie sandwiches are filled with red, white, and blue vanilla creme—whoopie, indeed!

Ingredients

6 tablespoons (3 oz/90 g) unsalted butter, at room temperature

½ cup (3½ oz/100 g) light brown sugar, firmly packed

1 large egg

1 teaspoon pure vanilla extract

¾ cup (4 oz/125 g) all-purpose flour

½ cup (1½ oz/45 g) natural cocoa powder

½ teaspoon baking soda

¼ teaspoon kosher salt

Vanilla Creme Filling

¼ cup (2 oz/60 g) unsalted butter, at room temperature

¾ cup (3 oz/90 g) confectioners' sugar

1 cup (8 oz/248 g) purchased marshmallow creme

½ teaspoon pure vanilla extract

Red and blue gel food coloring

★ In the bowl of a mixer fitted with the paddle attachment, beat the butter and sugar on medium-high speed until combined. Add the egg and vanilla and beat until blended. Sift the flour, cocoa, baking soda, and salt into the bowl and beat just until blended. Cover the bowl and refrigerate the dough until firm, about 2 hours.

★ Space 2 racks evenly in the oven and preheat to 350°F (180°C). Line 2 baking sheets with parchment.

★ With dampened hands, shape tablespoonfuls of the dough into balls. Place them firmly on the prepared pans, spacing them slightly apart and flattening them a little. You should have about 20 balls. Bake until the cookies are puffed and slightly firm, 8–10 minutes, rotating the pans about halfway through. Let the cookies cool on the pans for 5 minutes, then transfer to wire racks to cool completely.

★ Make the Vanilla Creme Filling: In the bowl of a mixer fitted with the paddle attachment, beat the butter and confectioners' sugar on medium-high speed until lightened. Stir in the marshmallow creme and vanilla extract on low speed until the filling is smooth. Divide the filling into 3 even parts; add a small amount of red gel food coloring to one portion of filling, until desired color is achieved. Repeat with blue food coloring in another portion of filling. Leave the third portion white.

★ Alternating colors for the different cookies, spread the flat side of half of the cookies with a big dollop of the filling. Or get creative and gently swirl together 2 or more filling colors. Top each with a second cookie, placing the flat side on the filling. Refrigerate until the filling is set, at least 1 hour.

Makes 10 mini whoopie pies

"For Spacious Skies" Pies

These coconut clouds, resting on a sky-blue candy glaze, are truly heavenly.

Ingredients

Nonstick cooking spray

3 large egg whites, at room temperature

¼ teaspoon cream of tartar

Pinch salt

¾ cup (6 oz/185 g) sugar

½ teaspoon pure vanilla extract

4½ cups (10 oz/150 g) sweetened shredded coconut

8 ounces (225 g) sky-blue candy coating pieces

★ Preheat the oven to 325°F (165°C). Line 3 baking sheets with parchment paper and lightly spray the paper with nonstick cooking spray.

★ In a clean, large bowl, combine the egg whites and cream of tartar. Using a mixer on medium-high speed, beat until the egg whites form a dense foam, about 1 minute. Add the salt. Beating continuously, gradually add the sugar and beat until stiff peaks form, 3–4 minutes. Using a rubber spatula, stir in the vanilla. In 3 batches, gently fold the coconut into the beaten whites, folding just until the coconut is incorporated. Place rounded tablespoonfuls of the dough on the prepared sheets, spacing them 1 inch (2.5 cm) apart.

★ Bake until the edges begin to turn lightly golden brown, 19–22 minutes. Let cool completely on the sheets, about 30 minutes.

★ Place the candy coating pieces in a microwave-safe silicone or plastic bowl. Microwave according to package directions, stirring occasionally, until melted and smooth.

★ Dip the bottom of each cookie into the coating and return to a parchment-lined sheet. Refrigerate until the coating is set, about 10 minutes. Store the cookies, in a single layer, in an airtight container at room temperature for up to 4 days.

Makes about 25 cookies

"Let Freedom Ring" Meringues

These delicious meringue spirals are pitch-perfect for those looking for a lighter treat.

Ingredients

1 cup (4 oz/125 g) confectioners' sugar

2 large egg whites, at room temperature

½ teaspoon salt

2 teaspoons pure vanilla extract

Colored sugar or nonpareils, for sprinkling

About 20 lollipop sticks

Specialty tools: Pastry bag with a ¼-inch (6-mm) round tip

★ Preheat the oven to 250°F (120°C). Line 3 large baking sheets with parchment paper. Trace twenty 2- to 3-inch (5- to 7.5-cm) circles on the paper; space rounds 1 inch (2.5 cm) apart, and leave room for the lollipop sticks. Then turn the paper over to avoid contact between the ink and batter.

★ Sift the sugar into a bowl. In a clean large bowl, using an electric mixer on medium-high speed, beat the egg whites until foamy, about 1 minute. Add the salt. Continue beating on medium-high speed until a dense foam forms, about 1 minute. Beating continuously, gradually add the sifted sugar, about 2 tablespoons at a time, until the sugar has been incorporated and the mixture is glossy and voluminous, 6–7 minutes. Add the vanilla extract and mix just until combined, about 1 minute more.

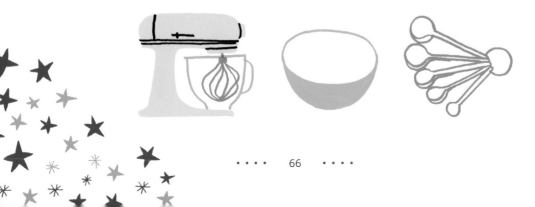

★ Spoon the egg white mixture into a large pastry bag with a ¼-inch (6-mm) round tip. Pipe the mixture onto the prepared baking sheets, starting in the center of each traced round and moving in circular pattern, working your way to the outer edge of the traced round. Sprinkle rounds with colored sugar or nonpareils and gently insert the lollipop sticks. Let stand at room temperature, uncovered, for 30 minutes.

★ Bake until the cookies feel firm and dry, 25–30 minutes. If they still feel tacky, turn off the oven and let them remain in the oven. Transfer to wire racks and let cool completely, about 30 minutes. When ready to serve, tie a patriotic ribbon around the lollipop stick.

★ Store in an airtight container, layered between sheets of parchment paper, in the refrigerator for up to 3 days.

Makes about 20 spirals

★ Tip: Replace the vanilla extract with the flavoring of your choice; almond, peppermint, or orange are all yummy options.

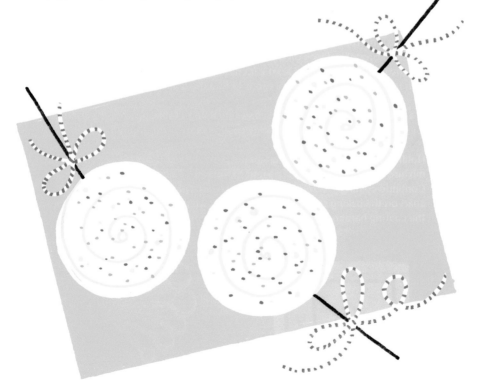

Patriotic Pretzels

Bright and bold, these pretzels are resplendent in red, blue, and white sprinkles—perfect for any party or event!

Ingredients

24 large pretzels

2 tablespoons solid shortening

½ cup (4 oz/120 g) royal blue candy coating pieces

½ cup (4 oz/120 g) white candy coating pieces

Assorted red, white, and blue nonpareils, jimmies, or other decorations

★ Line 2 baking sheets with parchment paper.

★ In a microwave-safe bowl, microwave 1 tablespoon of the shortening for 45 seconds. Add the blue candy coating pieces and stir until completely melted.

★ Holding a pretzel over the bowl, spoon the blue mixture over the pretzel until coated thoroughly. Place on baking sheet. Continue coating pretzels until 12 are covered. Space them at least 2 inches apart on the baking sheet. Sprinkle with red, white, and blue decorations before the coating hardens.

★ In a microwave-safe bowl, microwave remaining 1 tablespoon of the shortening for 45 seconds. Add the white candy coating pieces and stir until melted.

★ Holding one of the remaining uncoated pretzels over the bowl, spoon the white mixture over the pretzel until coated thoroughly. Place on baking sheet. Continue coating pretzels until 12 are covered. Space them at least 2 inches apart on the baking sheet. Sprinkle with red, white, and blue decorations before the coating hardens. Allow to set for 30 minutes before serving.

★ Store in an airtight container, layered between sheets of parchment paper, for up to one week.

Makes 24 pretzels

★ Tip: Dip the top three-quarters of pretzel rods into melted candy coating and roll them in sprinkles for an easy-to-hold treat. Wrap them in cellophane and display in a pretty jar or wide-mouthed vase.

I Scream for Freedom! Ice Cream Sandwiches

Everyone screams for ice cream when it's sandwiched between candy-laden cookies.

Ingredients

½ cup (4 oz/120 g) salted butter, at room temperature

6 tablespoons (3 oz/90 g) granulated sugar

6 tablespoons brown sugar (3 oz/90 g), firmly packed

1 egg

½ teaspoon vanilla extract

1 cup (4 oz/120 g) plus 2 tablespoons all-purpose flour

½ teaspoon baking soda

¼ teaspoon baking powder

Pinch salt

½ cup (1¾ oz/50 g) red and blue candy-coated chocolates

2 pints (32 oz/900 g) ice cream, in the flavor of your choice

Red, white, and blue nonpareils

★ Preheat oven to 350°F (180°C). Line 2 baking sheets with parchment.

★ In an electric mixer, cream together butter, granulated sugar, and brown sugar. Add egg and vanilla extract and beat on medium-high speed until light and fluffy. In a separate bowl, combine flour, baking soda, baking powder, and salt. Slowly add dry ingredients to wet ingredients, mixing well to incorporate after each addition. Fold in candy-coated chocolates.

★ Drop dough in generous spoonfuls onto prepared sheet, spacing cookies about 2 inches (5 cm) apart. Bake for 10–13 minutes, just until set (they should be slightly underbaked). Remove from oven and transfer to a wire rack. Cool completely.

★ Remove ice cream from freezer and let soften a little. Once cookies are cooled, scoop ice cream onto the bottom side of one cookie and top with another cookie. Gently press two cookies together until ice cream spreads to the edge of the cookie. Roll ice cream edges in nonpareils.

Makes 10–12 ice cream sandwiches

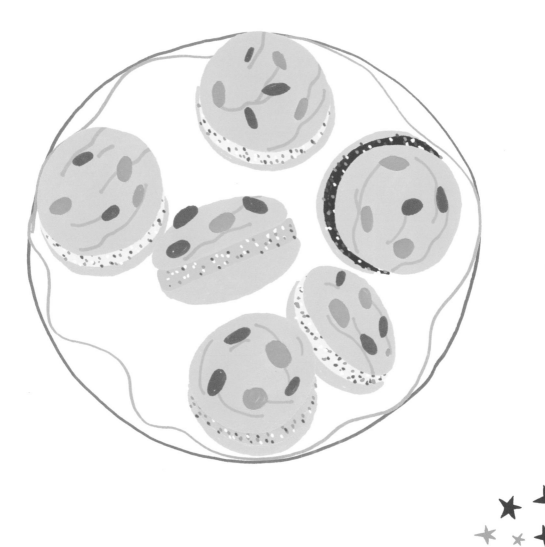

Bark for Your Park

This playful chocolate bark is packed with sweet and salty surprises—making it the perfect bake sale item for fundraisers in support of the environment or local parks.

Ingredients

Butter to grease baking sheet

8 ounces (250 g) white chocolate, finely chopped

¾ cup (4 oz/125 g) red, white, and blue candy-coated chocolates

¾ cup (4 oz/125 g) salted peanuts

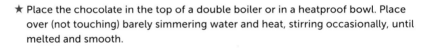

★ Butter a rimmed baking sheet and line with parchment paper.

★ Place the chocolate in the top of a double boiler or in a heatproof bowl. Place over (not touching) barely simmering water and heat, stirring occasionally, until melted and smooth.

★ Stir ½ cup (2½ oz/75 g) of the candies and ½ cup (2½ oz/75 g) of the peanuts into the melted chocolate, then pour onto the prepared baking sheet, tilting to spread slightly. Sprinkle with the remaining ¼ cup (1½ oz/45 g) each of the candies and peanuts. Refrigerate the bark, uncovered, until firm, about 1 hour.

★ Gently peel the candy from the parchment paper. Then, holding the candy with the parchment (to prevent fingerprints), break the chocolate into large, irregular pieces.

Makes about ¾ lb (375 g)

★ Tip: To punch up the connection to the environment, use green candies instead of patriotic colors, and stir in 3 tablespoons of flower-shaped candy confetti.

Peacestacio Bars

Sweet and tangy dried cranberries and citrus set off these crunchy, chewy pistachio bars. Go ahead, grab a peace!

Ingredients

Juice and finely grated zest of 2 medium oranges

1 cup (4 oz/125 g) unsalted, shelled pistachios

¾ cup (6 oz/180 g) granulated sugar

¾ cup (4 oz/125 g) all-purpose flour, plus more for dusting

1 teaspoon baking powder

½ teaspoon kosher salt

1 cup (6 oz/180 g) dried cranberries

¾ cup (6 oz/180 g) unsalted butter, at room temperature, plus more for greasing

3 large eggs

Confectioners' sugar, for dusting

★ Preheat the oven to 350°F (180°C). Generously butter a 7½-by-12-inch (19-by-30-cm) or 9-by-13-inch (23-by-33-cm) baking dish and dust with flour.

★ Strain the orange juice into a bowl and then measure ⅓ cup (3 fl oz/80 ml); set remainder aside for another use.

★ In a food processor, pulse the pistachios, orange zest, and half of the granulated sugar until finely ground. Put in a bowl and stir in the flour, baking powder, and salt. Mix in the cranberries.

★ In a mixer fitted with the paddle attachment, beat the butter and remaining sugar on medium-high speed until light and fluffy. Add the eggs one at a time, mixing well after each addition. Add the ⅓ cup juice. Gently stir in the cranberry-pistachio mixture just until combined.

★ Spread the batter in the prepared dish. Bake until light golden brown, about 30 minutes. Let cool in the dish for about 20 minutes, then turn out onto a wire rack set over a baking sheet to cool completely. Dust the top with confectioners' sugar and cut into bars. For fun packaging, wrap bars individually in parchment paper and secure with a peace sign sticker!

Makes about 18 bars

Care-amel Corn

Toss your popcorn with a sweet glaze of brown sugar, butter, and lots of TLC.

Ingredients

3 quarts (3 l) freshly popped corn (about ½ cup/3 oz/90 g unpopped)

1 cup (7 oz/220 g) dark brown sugar, firmly packed

½ cup (5 oz/155 ml) light corn syrup

½ cup (4 oz/125 g) unsalted butter, plus more for greasing

1 tablespoon finely grated orange zest

½ teaspoon kosher salt

1 teaspoon pure vanilla extract

½ teaspoon baking soda

Red, white, and blue candy confetti, such as stars (optional)

★ Preheat the oven to 250°F (120°C). Butter a large roasting pan. Spread the popcorn out in an even layer. Place the pan in the oven to warm while you make the caramel glaze.

★ In a large, heavy saucepan over medium heat, combine the brown sugar, corn syrup, butter, orange zest, and salt. Bring to a boil, stirring until the sugar dissolves. Boil for 4 minutes without stirring. Remove from the heat and stir in the vanilla and baking soda. Pour the hot glaze over the warm popcorn mixture and stir to coat. Sprinkle with candy confetti. Return the pan to the oven and bake, stirring occasionally, until the glaze is dry, about 1 hour.

★ Using a metal spatula, free the popcorn mixture from the bottom of the pan. Let cool completely in the pan, then break into clumps and serve. If you are selling this at a bake sale or other event, package in cellophane bags and tie with red, white, and blue curling ribbon.

Makes about 4 quarts

★ Tip: Add nuts and raisins or other dried fruit after the popcorn mixture has cooled to boost the nutrition (and flavor!) of this sweet treat.

CARE-AMEL
CORN

CHAPTER 4

America's Bread Winners— and Muffins and Cakes, Too!

Pilgrim Pride Bread

This spicy pumpkin quick bread is topped with cream cheese frosting. . . and a bright and berry-licous American flag.

Ingredients

Nonstick cooking spray

1 cup (8 oz/230 g) unsalted butter, at room temperature

1 cup (7 oz/200 g) granulated sugar

1 cup (7½ oz/215 g) brown sugar, firmly packed

4 eggs

1 15-ounce (425 g) can pumpkin puree

2 cups (8 oz/240 g) all-purpose flour

2 teaspoons ground cinnamon

2 teaspoons baking powder

1 teaspoon baking soda

½ teaspoon ground ginger

½ teaspoon ground cloves

2 cups (8 oz/240 g) raspberries

1½ cups (7½ oz/200 g) blueberries

Cream Cheese Frosting

1 package (8 oz/225 g) cream cheese, at room temperature

¼ cup (2 oz/60 g) unsalted butter, at room temperature

1 teaspoon vanilla

2 cups (8 oz/240 g) confectioners' sugar

★ Tip: You can use sliced strawberries in place of the raspberries, if you prefer—or mix the two.

★ Preheat oven to 350°F (180°C), and spray a 9-by-13 baking pan with nonstick cooking spray.

★ In the bowl of an electric mixer, cream together the butter, granulated sugar, and brown sugar. Add eggs and mix on high until well combined. Stir in pumpkin puree.

★ In a separate bowl, mix together flour, cinnamon, baking powder, baking soda, ginger, and cloves. Add dry ingredients to the mixing bowl with the wet ingredients in three parts, stirring after each addition until just mixed. Pour batter into prepared pan and bake for 25–30 minutes, until golden. Remove from oven and let cool completely.

★ Make the Cream Cheese Frosting: In a mixing bowl, stir together cream cheese, butter, and vanilla. Slowly mix in confectioners' sugar until smooth.

★ Spread Cream Cheese Frosting onto the pumpkin bread, reserving a tablespoon if you would like to create "stars" on your flag. Arrange blueberries in a square in upper left corner to represent the field of blue in the American flag; arrange raspberries in double rows to represent the flag's stripes. If desired, dot reserved Cream Cheese Frosting on the blueberries to represent the flag's stars. Store covered in refrigerator until ready to serve.

Makes 24 servings

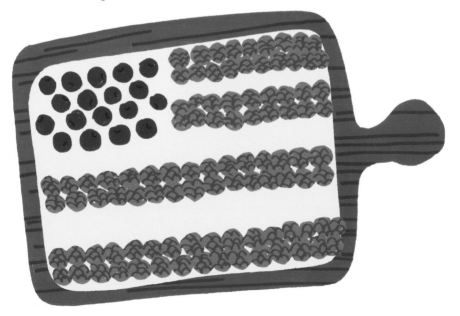

No Meanies Zucchini Bread

Work vegetables into your baked goods to make healthful treats. Work kindness and respect into your life to make a better world. This delightful quick and easy zucchini bread is sure to be popular with adults and kids alike.

Ingredients

Nonstick cooking spray

½ cup (4 oz/120 g) unsalted butter, at room temperature

½ cup (3½ oz/100 g) brown sugar, firmly packed

1 egg

1 teaspoon pure vanilla extract

⅓ cup sour cream (3 oz/80 g)

1½ cup (6½ oz/190 g) whole wheat flour

1 teaspoon cinnamon

1 teaspoon baking powder

½ teaspoon baking soda

Pinch salt

1 cup (8 oz/150 g) finely grated zucchini, about 3 small

★ Preheat oven to 350°F (180°C), and spray an 8-by-4-inch (20-by-10-cm) loaf pan with nonstick cooking spray.

★ In the bowl of an electric mixer, cream together the butter and sugar. Add the egg and vanilla extract and mix until fluffy. Mix in sour cream.

★ In a separate bowl, mix together flour, cinnamon, baking powder, baking soda, and salt. Add dry ingredients to the bowl with the wet ingredients in three parts, stirring with each addition until just incorporated. Stir zucchini into the batter.

★ Pour batter into the prepared loaf pan and bake for 45–55 minutes, until a toothpick inserted in the center comes out clean. Remove from oven and cool on wire rack 10 minutes. Loosen sides of loaf from pan and remove from pan. Transfer to a wire rack and allow to cool slightly before slicing and serving. Or cool completely and wrap in parchment paper tied with red and blue ribbon or secured with tape in a patriotic design!

Makes 8 servings

We Love OutCiders Muffins

Sprinkled generously with cinnamon streusel—and with a sweet streak hidden inside—these quick and easy apple cider muffins will become a favorite of all.

Ingredients

1¾ cups (9 oz/280 g) all-purpose flour

2 teaspoons baking powder

¼ teaspoon salt

¼ cup (2 oz/60 g) granulated sugar

1 egg, beaten

¾ cup (6 fl oz/180 ml) apple cider or apple juice

¼ cup (2 fl oz/60 ml) vegetable oil or butter

Streusel Topping

⅓ cup (2½ oz/75 g) dark brown sugar, firmly packed

3 tablespoons all-purpose flour

2 teaspoons ground cinnamon

3 tablespoons cold unsalted butter

★ Preheat the oven to 400°F (200°C). Grease 12 standard muffin cups or line them with paper or foil liners.

★ In a large mixing bowl, sift together the flour, baking powder, and salt. Stir in the granulated sugar. Make a well in the center.

★ In a small mixing bowl, combine the egg, cider, and oil. Add all at once to the flour mixture and stir until just moistened (the batter should be lumpy).

★ Make the Streusel Topping: In a small mixing bowl, stir together the brown sugar, flour, and cinnamon. Using a pastry blender or two knives held crosswise, cut in the butter until the mixture resembles coarse crumbs.

★ Spoon about 1 tablespoon of batter into each prepared muffin cup, sprinkle with 1 teaspoon of the streusel mixture, and continue to fill the cups with the remaining batter until they're two-thirds full. Sprinkle the tops evenly with the remaining streusel.

★ Bake until the muffins are golden brown and a wooden toothpick inserted into the center of one comes out clean, about 15 minutes. Remove from the oven and cool in the pan for 5 minutes. Serve warm, or transfer the muffins to a wire rack to cool.

Makes 12 standard muffins

No Bluffin' Muffins

What the world needs now is more "realness"—so let's all be real! Enjoy these straightforward, protein-packed muffins and give your body what it needs. Give your brain the same respect: live in a world where truth and facts matter. (How's that for sage advice?)

Ingredients

¼ cup (2 fl oz/60 ml) plus 1 tablespoon extra-virgin olive oil

¼ pound (4 oz/125 g) fresh Italian sausage, casing well pricked

2 cups (10 oz/315 g) self-rising flour

½ teaspoon baking powder

2 eggs, lightly beaten

1 cup (8 fl oz/250 ml) milk

2 tablespoons finely shredded fresh sage leaves

★ Preheat the oven to 400°F (200°C). Grease 12 standard muffin cups or line them with paper liners.

★ In a medium frying pan over medium-high heat, warm 1 tablespoon of the olive oil. Add the sausage and sauté, turning occasionally to brown evenly, until cooked through, about 15 minutes. Remove from the pan, drain on paper towels, and leave to cool. When cool, peel off the casing and finely crumble the meat. Set aside.

★ In a large mixing bowl, sift together the flour and baking powder. Make a well in the center.

★ In a small mixing bowl, combine the eggs, milk, and remaining oil. Add all at once to the flour mixture, together with the crumbled sausage and the sage. Stir until just moistened (the batter should be lumpy).

★ Spoon the batter into the prepared muffin cups, filling them two-thirds full. Bake until the muffins are golden brown and a wooden toothpick inserted into the center of one comes out clean, 15–20 minutes. Remove from the oven and cool in the pan for 5 minutes. Serve warm, or transfer the muffins to a wire rack to cool.

Makes 12 standard muffins

★ Tip: Either spicy or sweet Italian sausage is delicious in this recipe—or substitute any flavorful fresh sausage.

Red, White, and Blueberry Bread

This whole-grain quick bread bursts with the bright, juicy flavors of summer.

Ingredients

Nonstick cooking spray

1 cup (5 oz/155 g) processed wheat bran

1 cup (8 oz/250 ml) skim milk

½ cup (4 oz/125 g) unsalted butter, at room temperature

1 cup (7 oz/220 g) light brown sugar, lightly packed

1 egg

2 cups (10 oz/315 g) whole-wheat self-rising flour

1 teaspoon baking powder

½ cup (2½ oz/90 g) fresh or frozen blueberries

½ cup (2 oz/60 g) fresh or frozen raspberries

★ Preheat the oven to 350°F (150°C). Coat an 8½-by-4½-inch (22-by-11.5-cm) loaf pan with nonstick cooking spray.

★ Put the bran and milk in a bowl and leave at room temperature until all of the liquid is absorbed, about 30 minutes.

★ In a mixing bowl, using a hand-held electric mixer on high speed, cream together the butter and sugar until light and fluffy. Beat in the egg. Add the bran mixture. Sift together the flour and baking powder, then fold them into the butter-and-sugar mixture, mixing well. Gently stir in the blueberries and raspberries just until evenly distributed.

★ Spoon the batter into the prepared pan. Bake until the loaf is golden brown and a wooden toothpick inserted into the center comes out clean, 1 hour– 1 hour 10 minutes. Remove from the oven and cool in the pan for 10 minutes. Loosen loaf from sides of pan and remove from pan. Serve warm, or transfer to a wire rack to cool.

Makes 8 servings

Raisin' Good Kids Oat Muffins

Flavorful oat muffins are packed with ripe banana and golden raisins, for a healthy, happy start to any day.

Ingredients

2 cups (10 oz/315 g) self-rising flour

1 teaspoon ground cinnamon

½ teaspoon baking soda

1 cup (3 oz/90 g) rolled oats, plus ⅓ cup (1 oz/30 g) extra

½ cup (3 oz/90 g) golden raisins

½ cup (3½ oz/105 g) dark brown sugar, firmly packed

2 eggs, lightly beaten

¾ cup (6 oz/180 ml) milk

¼ cup (2 oz/60 ml) vegetable oil

2 very ripe medium bananas, mashed (to yield about 1 cup/8 oz/250 g)

½ cup (3½ oz/110 g) Demerara sugar

★ Preheat the oven to 400°F (200°C). Grease 6 large (1-cup/250-ml) muffin cups or line them with paper liners.

★ In a large mixing bowl, sift together the flour, cinnamon, and baking soda. Stir in the 1 cup (3 oz/90 g) of oats, the raisins, and the brown sugar. Make a well in the center.

★ In a small mixing bowl, combine the eggs, milk, oil, and banana. Add all at once to the oat mixture and stir until just moistened (the batter should be lumpy).

★ Spoon the batter into the prepared muffin cups, filling them two-thirds full. Sprinkle with the Demerara sugar and the extra rolled oats.

★ Bake until the muffins are golden brown and a wooden toothpick inserted into the center of one comes out clean, 25–30 minutes. Remove the muffins from the oven and cool them in the pan for 5 minutes. Serve warm, or transfer to a wire rack to cool.

Makes 6 large muffins

Bites for Your Rights Mini Scones

Every bake sale needs something savory, like these bite-sized bacon and sharp Cheddar scones.

Ingredients

3 thick slices applewood-smoked bacon

2 cups (10 oz/315 g) all-purpose flour

1 cup (4 oz/125 g) shredded sharp Cheddar cheese

2 teaspoons baking powder

Pinch kosher salt

½ teaspoon freshly ground pepper

½ cup (4 oz/125 g) cold unsalted butter, cut into chunks

1 large egg

¾ cup (6 fl oz/180 ml) heavy cream or whole milk

2 tablespoons chopped fresh chives

★ Preheat the oven to 400°F (200°C). Line a rimmed baking sheet with parchment paper.

★ In a frying pan, fry the bacon over medium-low heat until lightly crisp, about 5 minutes. Transfer to a cutting board and finely chop the bacon.

★ In a food processor, combine the flour, cheese, baking powder, salt, and pepper and pulse briefly to mix. Add the butter and pulse until the mixture looks like coarse meal. In a small bowl, whisk together the egg and cream until blended. Pour the egg mixture into the processor and pulse just until the dough comes together.

★ Dump the dough onto a lightly floured work surface. Knead in the bacon and chives, just until distributed, and then bring the dough together into a ball. Using a floured rolling pin, roll out the dough to ½ inch (12 mm) thick. Using a 1½-inch (4-cm) biscuit cutter, cut out as many scones as you can. Gather the scraps of dough, roll out, and cut out more scones.

★ Space the scones evenly on the prepared baking sheet. Bake until the scones are golden, about 12 minutes. Remove from the pan and let cool slightly on a wire rack before serving.

Makes about 4 dozen mini scones

We the people...

Free Speech Peach Cake

Everyone will speak highly of this peachy-keen streusel coffee cake!

Ingredients

1½ cups (7½ oz/235 g) all-purpose flour

¾ cup (6 oz/185 g) granulated sugar

2 teaspoons baking powder

½ teaspoon salt

1 large egg

4 tablespoons (2 oz/60 g) unsalted butter, melted

½ cup (4 fl oz/125 ml) milk

1½ teaspoons vanilla extract

1 teaspoon almond extract

2 firm, ripe peaches, about 1 pound (500 g) total, peeled pitted, and sliced 1 inch (2.5 cm) thick

Streusel Topping

¾ cup (4 oz/125 g) all-purpose flour

⅓ cup (2½ oz/75 g) light brown sugar, firmly packed

¼ cup (2 oz/60 g) granulated sugar

1 teaspoon ground cinnamon

6 tablespoons (3 oz/90 g) cold unsalted butter, cut into small pieces

★ Preheat the oven to 350°F (180°C). Grease and flour a 9-inch (23-cm) round springform pan or baking dish.

★ In a bowl, stir together the flour, sugar, baking powder, and salt.

★ In another bowl, using an electric mixer on medium speed or a wire whisk, beat the egg, melted butter, milk, and vanilla and almond extracts until creamy, about 1 minute. Add to the dry ingredients and beat just until evenly moistened. There should be no lumps or dry spots. Do not overmix.

★ Spoon the batter into the prepared pan and spread evenly. Arrange the peach slices in concentric circles from the pan sides to the center. Gently press the slices into the batter.

★ Make the Streusel Topping: Stir together the flour, brown and granulated sugars, and cinnamon in a bowl. Using a pastry cutter or your fingers, cut or rub in the butter until coarse crumbs form.

★ Sprinkle the streusel evenly over the cake batter and bake until the topping is golden brown, 40–45 minutes. A toothpick inserted into the center of the cake should come out clean. Transfer the pan to a wire rack and let cool for 20 minutes. Remove the sides of the springform pan, if using. Serve warm or at room temperature, cut into wedges.

Makes one 9-inch (23-cm) cake

★ Note: if using a glass baking dish, reduce the oven temperature to 325°F (165°C).

Brans Against Bans

These honey-kissed raisin bran muffins are healthful reminders of everything we stand for—a country open to all, regardless of religion.

Ingredients

2 cups (10 oz/315 g) all-purpose flour

2 cups (8 oz/250 g) unprocessed bran flakes

1½ cups (9 oz/280 g) mixed dark and golden raisins

⅓ cup (1 oz/30 g) toasted wheat germ

2 teaspoons baking soda

1 teaspoon baking powder

1 teaspoon salt

½ cup (4 oz/125 g) unsalted butter, at room temperature

½ cup (3½ oz/105 g) light or dark brown sugar, firmly packed

½ cup (6 oz/185 g) honey

1 cup (8 oz/250 g) plain yogurt

½ cup (4 fl oz/125 ml) buttermilk

2 teaspoons vanilla extract

3 large eggs, beaten

★ Preheat the oven to 400°F (200°C). Grease 18 standard muffin cups with butter or butter-flavored nonstick cooking spray; fill the unused cups one-third full with water to prevent warping.

★ In a bowl, stir together the flour, bran, raisins, wheat germ, baking soda, baking powder, and salt.

★ In another bowl, using a wooden spoon, cream together the butter, brown sugar, and honey until fluffy. Beat in the yogurt, then the buttermilk and vanilla, until well blended and smooth.

★ Make a well in the center of the dry ingredients and add the creamed mixture and the eggs. Beat just until evenly moistened. The batter will be thick and slightly lumpy. Do not overmix.

★ Spoon the batter into each muffin cup, filling it level with the rim of the cup.

★ Transfer the filled pan(s) to the oven and immediately reduce the oven temperature to 350°F (180°C). Bake until golden, dry, and springy to the touch, 18–22 minutes. A toothpick inserted into the center of a muffin should come out clean. Transfer the pan(s) to wire racks and let cool for at least 15 minutes. Unmold the muffins. Serve warm or at room temperature, with butter.

Makes 18 muffins

Everyone's Welcrumb Cake

Everyone is surely welcome to a slice
of this delectable raspberry crumb cake!

Ingredients

1¾ cups (9 oz/380 g) all-purpose flour

1 cup (8 oz/250 g) granulated sugar

2 teaspoons baking powder

½ teaspoon baking soda

¼ teaspoon salt

3 large eggs

1 cup (8 oz/250 g) sour cream

1 teaspoon vanilla extract

2 cups (8 oz/250 g) fresh raspberries

2 tablespoons confectioners' sugar

Crumb Topping

1 cup (5 oz/155 g) all-purpose (plain) flour

⅔ cup (5 oz/155 g) granulated sugar

Grated zest of 1 lemon

½ cup (4 oz/125 g) unsalted butter, melted

★ Preheat the oven to 350°F (180°C). Grease and flour a 10-inch (25-cm) round springform pan.

★ In a bowl, stir together the flour, sugar, baking powder, baking soda, and salt.

★ In another bowl, whisk together the eggs, sour cream, and vanilla until well blended. Make a well in the center of the dry ingredients and add the sour cream mixture. Beat until smooth and fluffy, about 2 minutes.

★ Spoon the batter into the prepared pan and spread evenly. Cover evenly with the raspberries.

★ Make the Crumb Topping: Stir together the flour, sugar, and zest in a small bowl. Add the melted butter and stir with a fork until the mixture is crumbly.

★ Sprinkle the crumb topping evenly over the berries and bake until the topping is golden brown, 38–42 minutes. A toothpick inserted into the center of the cake should come out clean. Transfer the pan to a wire rack and let cool for 20 minutes. Remove the sides of the springform pan. Dust with the confectioners' sugar and serve warm or at room temperature, cut into wedges.

Makes one 10-inch (25-cm) cake

CHAPTER 5

Freedom Fighters

Chocolate Dream Cake

So many of us—or our ancestors—came to America with a
dream. Anything is possible in the U.S.A.! (Even a truly
decadent gluten-free chocolate torte.)

Ingredients

1 cup (6 oz/185 g) dried sour cherries

3 tablespoons aged balsamic vinegar or brandy

12 ounces (375 g) bittersweet (60%) chocolate, chopped,
or bittersweet chocolate chips

¾ cup (6 oz/185 g) unsalted butter, cut into small pieces

6 large eggs

1 cup (7 oz/220 g) packed brown sugar

4 tablespoons (2 oz /60 g) granulated sugar

¼ teaspoon kosher salt

Confectioners' sugar, for dusting

Fresh cherries, for topping (optional)

Whipped cream, for serving (optional)

★ In a small bowl, combine dried cherries and vinegar and let soak for 2 hours.

★ Preheat the oven to 350°F (180°C). Butter a 9-inch (23-cm) springform pan and
line the bottom with a round of parchment paper. Wrap the outside of the
pan tightly with 3 layers of heavy-duty aluminum foil, covering the bottom
and sides completely.

★ In the top of a double boiler set over (not touching) simmering water, combine
the chocolate and butter. Heat, stirring often, until the chocolate and butter
are melted and smooth. Remove the bowl from over the water.

★ In a large bowl, whisk together the eggs, brown sugar, and granulated sugar
until well blended. Gradually add the chocolate mixture, whisking until smooth.
Stir in the salt and then the cherry mixture. Scrape the batter into the prepared
pan and shake gently to level the top of the batter.

★ Bring a kettle of water to a boil. Place the cake pan in a large roasting pan and add enough hot water to the roasting pan to rise halfway up the sides of the cake pan. Cover the cake pan with aluminum foil but do not fold down the edges.

★ Bake the cake until set in the center and the outer edge is dry to the touch, about 1 hour 40 minutes. Carefully remove the cake pan from the roasting pan and strip the foil from the cake pan. Transfer the cake to a wire rack to cool completely in the cake pan, about 2 hours. Cover and refrigerate the cake until chilled, at least 3 hours and up to 3 days.

★ To serve, remove the sides of the springform pan and transfer the cake to a platter. Dust the cake with confectioners' sugar, then cut into thin wedges. Add a dollop of whipped cream and a cherry. Serve chilled or at room temperature.

Makes 12 servings

★ Tip: For extra flair, use parchment paper to create a decorative stencil—simply cut your pattern in the paper, lay it on the cake top, and dust confectioners' sugar over the parchment paper, then lift the paper carefully from both sides at once.

Chipping-in Scones

These dairy-free, nut-free, vegan scones let those with food allergies or preferences join in the treat-filled fun.

Ingredients

1 tablespoon flaxseed meal

¾ cup (180 ml) unsweetened plain almond milk

¾ cup (3 oz/90 g) spelt flour

1¼ cups (5 oz/150 g) unbleached all-purpose flour

1 tablespoons baking powder

¼ cup (1¾ oz/50 g) sugar, plus more for topping

½ teaspoon sea salt

6 tablespoons (3 oz/80 g) coconut oil, in solid form, or vegan butter

⅓ cup (2 oz/60 g) vegan chocolate chips

★ Preheat the oven to 400°F (200°C). Line a baking sheet with parchment paper.

★ Prepare a "flax egg": In a small mixing bowl, mix together the flaxseed meal and 2½ tablespoons water and allow to set for 5 minutes.

★ Add almond milk to the flax egg and stir to combine. In a separate mixing bowl, add spelt flour, all-purpose flour, baking powder, ¼ cup sugar, and salt. Whisk to combine.

★ Stir the coconut oil (at cool room temperature, the oil should be solid rather than liquid or half-solid) into the dry ingredients, and use a pastry cutter (or two knives, working criss-cross) to cut in the oil until the mixture resembles coarse crumbs. Stir the flax-almond milk mixture again and add a little at a time, stirring with a mixing spoon until a dough forms. Gently fold in chocolate chips.

★ Transfer dough to a floured surface and use your hands to form a disc about 6–7 inches (15–18 cm) in diameter and 1 inch (2.5 cm) in height. Use a large knife to cut the disc into 6 wedges, as you would a pie. Use a floured spatula to transfer the scones to the prepared baking sheet, and sprinkle the tops with sugar.

★ Bake for 22–27 minutes, or until fluffy and golden at the edges. Serve warm or at room temperature. Scones are best when fresh, but can be stored at room temperature in an airtight container for up to 3 days.

Makes 6 scones

We Shall Overcrumb Cake

Calling all gluten-free bakers! Now you can overcome your craving for crumb cake with some buttery, nutmeg-spiked, and apple-laden goodness.

Ingredients

1½ cups (7 oz/160 g) sorghum flour

1 cup (7 oz/220 g) brown sugar, firmly packed

½ cup (1½ oz/45 g) almond meal

½ cup (2½ oz/75 g) potato starch

2 teaspoons ground cinnamon

1½ teaspoons xanthan gum

1¼ teaspoons baking powder

1 teaspoon baking soda

¾ teaspoon kosher salt

1 cup (8 oz/250 g) plain yogurt

3 large eggs

½ cup (4 fl oz/125 ml) oil or melted butter

1 tablespoon pure vanilla extract

1½ cups (6 oz/180 g) peeled and finely diced apples (about 1 medium)

Crumb Topping

½ cup (1¾ oz/55 g) sorghum flour

½ cup (3½ oz/105 g) brown sugar, firmly packed

¾ teaspoon ground cinnamon

¼ teaspoon ground nutmeg

¼ teaspoon kosher salt

¼ cup (2 oz/60 g) cold unsalted butter, cut into ½-inch (12-mm) pieces

★ Tip: For a nut-free version, make this cake with millet flour in place of the almond meal (it is almost as good).

★ Preheat the oven to 350°F (180°C). Line a 9-inch (23-cm) square baking pan with parchment paper.

★ In a large bowl, whisk together the sorghum flour, brown sugar, almond meal, potato starch, cinnamon, xanthan gum, baking powder, baking soda, and salt. In a separate bowl, whisk together the yogurt, eggs, oil, and vanilla extract. Add the liquid ingredients to the dry ingredients and stir until smooth. Fold in the apples. Scrape the batter into the prepared pan.

★ Make the Crumb Topping: In a food processor, pulse the sorghum flour, brown sugar, cinnamon, nutmeg, and salt until blended. Add the butter and pulse until the mixture begins to form clumps.

★ Spoon the topping evenly over the batter. Bake the cake until springy to the touch and a toothpick inserted into the center comes out clean, about 45 minutes. Let cool on a wire rack for at least 40 minutes. Cut into squares or rectangles. Serve warm or at room temperature.

Makes about 10 servings

Chocolate "No Wall" Nut Brownies

Bake these gooey, gluten-free brownies sans "wall-nuts"—
be creative and choose your own favorite add-ins.

Ingredients

8 ounces (250 g) bittersweet or semisweet chocolate, chopped

6 tablespoons (3 oz/90 g) unsalted butter, cut into pieces

¾ cup (6 oz/185 g) brown sugar, firmly packed

2 large eggs

1 teaspoon pure vanilla extract

2 tablespoons unsweetened cocoa powder

1 tablespoons sorghum flour

1 tablespoon tapioca flour or potato starch

⅛ teaspoon kosher salt

1 cup (4 oz/125 g) almonds, toasted and coarsely chopped

★ Preheat the oven to 350°F (180°C). Line an 8-inch (20-cm)
   square baking pan with foil, letting some excess foil extend
   up 2 opposite sides of the pan. Butter the foil.

★ In a saucepan over low heat, melt the chocolate and butter until smooth, stirring
   constantly. Remove the pan from the heat, add the brown sugar, and stir well.
   Stir in the eggs, 1 at a time, then stir in the vanilla extract. Add the cocoa powder,
   sorghum flour, tapioca flour, and salt and whisk vigorously until the batter is silky
   and no longer grainy, at least 1 minute. Stir in the almonds. Scrape the batter
   into the prepared pan.

★ Bake until the brownies are just set in the center and a toothpick inserted into the center comes out with moist crumbs, 25–30 minutes. Let the brownies cool completely in the pan on a wire rack.

★ Holding the ends of the foil, lift the brownies onto a cutting surface. Peel back the foil sides. Using a large, sharp knife, cut into 12 rectangles. Store at room temperature, covered with foil, for up to 3 days, or freeze for up to 1 month.

Makes 1 dozen brownies

★ Tip: Swap in your favorite nuts for the almonds—or add chocolate chips, peanut butter chips, or dried fruit for your own take on these delectable brownies.

"Be Your Best" Nests

These dreamy meringue nests are filled with sweet vanilla cream and juicy summer berries—but no gluten!

Ingredients

4 large egg whites, at room temperature

¼ teaspoon cream of tartar

1¼ cups (10 oz/300 g) sugar

1 teaspoon pure vanilla extract

Pinch kosher salt

2 cups (8 oz/250 g) fresh strawberries, stemmed and quartered lengthwise

2 cups (8 oz/250 g) fresh blueberries

Dark chocolate shavings (optional)

Vanilla Cream Filling

1 cup heavy cream

½ cup plain nonfat Greek yogurt

2 teaspoons vanilla bean paste or pure vanilla extract

2 tablespoons granulated sugar

★ Tip: Make the meringues the day before you want to serve them, so they have plenty of time to dry out.

★ Place racks in the upper and lower thirds of the oven and preheat to 200°F (95°C). Line 2 large baking sheets with parchment paper.

★ In a stand mixer, beat the egg whites on medium speed until frothy. Add the cream of tartar and beat on medium-high speed until soft peaks form, about 2 minutes. Gradually add 1 cup (8 oz/250 g) of the sugar, 1 tablespoon at a time, beating constantly. Add the vanilla and salt and continue beating until stiff and glossy and the egg whites hold a peak when the beater is lifted straight up, 1–2 minutes longer.

★ Immediately spoon the meringue in 8 mounds about ½ cup (4 fl oz/125 ml) each onto prepared baking sheets. Using the back of a metal spoon, gently create a ¾ inch (2 cm) deep, wide well in the center of each mound.

★ Bake the meringues until dry and crisp, about 2 hours, switching the baking sheets halfway though. Turn off the oven and let the meringues cool completely in the closed oven, about 2 hours.

★ Make the Vanilla Cream Filling: Combine the cream, yogurt, vanilla bean paste, and sugar in the bowl of a stand mixer with the whisk attachment on high speed. Beat until soft peaks form, about 2–3 minutes.

★ Spoon about 3 tablespoons of Vanilla Cream Filling into each meringue nest and top with strawberries and blueberries. Sprinkle with dark chocolate shavings, if desired, and serve at once.

Makes 8 nests

Biscotti Banners

Fly these "banners" proudly, and let everyone know that these delicious treats are dairy free and nut free.

Ingredients

2 cups (10 oz/315 g) all-purpose flour

1 teaspoon baking powder

¼ teaspoon baking soda

⅛ teaspoon kosher salt

2 large eggs

½ cup (4 fl oz/ 125 ml) canola oil

⅔ cup (8 oz/250 g) maple syrup

⅓ cup (3 oz/90 g) sugar

Finely grated zest of 1 orange

1 cup (6 oz/180 g) dried cranberries

1 cup (6 oz/180 g) dried blueberries

1 large egg white beaten with 1 teaspoon water

1 cup (6 oz/180 g) vegan dark chocolate, chopped

Red, white, and blue jimmies or star sprinkles

★ In a bowl, sift together the flour, baking powder, baking soda, and salt. In a large bowl, whisk together the eggs, oil, maple syrup, sugar, and zest. Add the dry ingredients and stir to combine. Stir in the dried cranberries and blueberries. Cover the bowl and refrigerate the dough for at least 2 hours.

★ Preheat the oven to 350°F (180°C). Line 2 baking sheets with parchment paper.

★ Divide the dough in half. With wet hands, shape each portion into a long, thin log about 15 inches (38 cm) long and 2 inches (5 cm) wide. Place the logs on one of the prepared pans, spacing them evenly (they will spread quite a bit). Brush the tops and sides lightly with the egg wash. Bake until golden, about 20 minutes. Let cool for about 15 minutes.

★ Cut the logs crosswise into slices about ½ inch (12 mm) thick. Carefully lay the slices, cut side down, on the prepared pans. Space 2 oven racks evenly in the oven and reduce the temperature to 325°F (165°C). Bake the biscotti until toasted and crisp, about 15 minutes, turning the biscotti once and rotating the baking sheets about halfway through. Let the biscotti cool on the pans for 5 minutes, then transfer to wire racks to cool completely.

★ Melt the chocolate in a double boiler or in a metal bowl set over a pot of simmering water on the stovetop. Dip top half of biscotti into the melted chocolate, and then sprinkle liberally with red, white, and blue jimmies. Store in an airtight container, layered between sheets of parchment paper, at room temperature for up to one week.

Makes about 4 dozen biscotti

Bananas for Liberty

You'll go bananas for this delicious gluten-free, dairy-free, and vegan quick bread.

Ingredients

1 tablespoon flaxseed meal

3 ripe medium bananas, about 1½ cups (12½ oz/350 g)

½ cup (3½ oz/100 g) brown sugar, firmly packed

3 tablespoons grape-seed oil or melted coconut oil

2–3 tablespoons maple syrup

¾ cup (6 fl oz/180 ml) unsweetened almond milk

1¼ cups (4⅓ oz/123 g) almond meal

1¼ cups (6¾ oz/190 g) gluten-free flour blend

1¼ cups (4⅓ oz/123 g) gluten-free oats

3½ teaspoons baking powder

¾ teaspoon sea salt

½ teaspoon ground cinnamon

★ Preheat the oven to 350°F (176°C). Line a 9-by-5-inch (23-by-13-cm) loaf pan with parchment paper.

★ Prepare a "flax egg": In a small bowl, mix together the flaxseed meal and 2½ tablespoons of water and allow to thicken for 5 minutes.

★ Mash bananas in a large bowl. In a separate bowl, mix together the flax egg, brown sugar, oil, and maple syrup and whisk until combined. Gradually whisk in almond milk, and then the bananas. Add almond meal, flour blend, oats, salt, and cinnamon and mix just until incorporated; do not overmix.

★ Bake for 1 hour and check for doneness; when ready, the loaf should feel firm and be crackly and golden brown on top. Bake up to 15 additional minutes. Let cool completely before cutting, or the loaf will not hold its form.

★ Wrap slices in individual wax paper bags and secure with decorative tape, a patriotic sticker, or ribbons! Store leftovers in an airtight container for up to three days.

Makes 9 servings

Cinnamon Soldiers

These sweet, gooey cinnamon rolls are perfect for the bake sale nut-free win. Support our country's veterans and truly Bake America Great Again by paying tribute to those who have fought—and continue to battle bravely—on our nation's behalf.

Ingredients

1 package (2¼ tsp) active dry yeast

¾ cup (6 fl oz /180 ml) whole milk, warmed

¼ cup (4 oz/125 g) granulated sugar

4 large eggs

4½ cups (22½ oz/705 g) all-purpose flour, plus more as needed

1½ teaspoons kosher salt

6 tablespoons (3 oz/80 g) unsalted butter, at room temperature, cut into chunks

Cinnamon Filling

4 tablespoons (2 oz/60 g) unsalted butter, at room temperature, cut into chunks

⅔ cup (5 oz/155 g) light brown sugar, firmly packed

2 teaspoons ground cinnamon

1 egg lightly beaten with 1 teaspoon water

Glaze

1 cup (4 oz/120 g) confectioners' sugar

1–2 tablespoons whole milk

★ In the bowl of a stand mixer, dissolve the yeast in the warm milk and let stand until foamy, about 10 minutes. Add the granulated sugar, eggs, 4½ cups flour, and salt. Attach the dough hook and knead on low speed, adding a little more flour if needed, until the ingredients come together. Add the butter and continue to knead until the dough is smooth and springy, about 7 minutes. Lightly oil a large bowl. Form the dough into a ball, put it in the oiled bowl, and cover the bowl with plastic wrap. Let the dough rise at room temperature until it doubles, 1½–2 hours.

★ Butter a 9-by-13-inch (23-by-33-cm) baking dish. Punch down the dough and turn out onto a lightly floured work surface. Cut it in half. Roll out 1 dough half into a rectangle about 9 by 14 inches (23 by 35 cm).

★ Make the Cinnamon Filling: Spread the dough with half of the butter, then sprinkle evenly with half of the brown sugar and half of the cinnamon. Starting at the long side closest to you, roll the rectangle away from you, forming a log. Cut the log crosswise into 8 equal slices. Arrange the slices, cut side down, in half of the prepared pan.

★ Repeat with the remaining dough and filling ingredients, and arrange the slices in the other half of the pan. Cover the pan loosely with plastic wrap and let stand in a warm, draft-free spot until puffy, about 1 hour, or refrigerate overnight, then let stand at room temperature for 30–60 minutes before baking.

★ Make the Glaze: Mix together confectioners' sugar and milk in a small bowl until well combined.

★ Preheat oven to 400°F (200°C). Brush the buns lightly with the beaten egg. Bake until the rolls are golden brown and a toothpick inserted into the center of a roll comes out clean, 20–25 minutes. Let the rolls cool slightly in the pan on a wire rack, then drizzle with the Glaze while they are still warm. Pull the rolls apart, top with an American flag, and enjoy.

Makes 16 rolls

Never-Judgy Fudgy Meringues

Don't worry—we won't judge! These gluten-free, nut-free fudgy meringues are so delicious you won't be able to eat just one.

Ingredients

4 ounces (125 g) bittersweet chocolate, chopped

2 large egg whites, at room temperature

⅛ teaspoon cream of tartar

½ cup (4 oz/125 g) sugar

½ teaspoon pure vanilla extract

⅛ teaspoon kosher salt

½ cup (1½ oz/45 g) shredded unsweetened coconut

★ Preheat the oven to 325°F (165°C). Line a large baking sheet with parchment paper.

★ Place the chocolate in the top of a double boiler set over (not touching) simmering water. Stir until melted and smooth. Remove from over the water and let cool slightly.

★ In a stand mixer, beat the egg whites on medium speed until frothy, about 2 minutes. Add the cream of tartar and beat on medium-high speed until soft peaks form, about 2 minutes. Gradually add the sugar, 1 tablespoon at a time, beating until the whites are stiff, about 3 minutes. Beat in the vanilla and salt just until incorporated. Using a rubber spatula, gently fold in the shredded coconut, followed by the melted chocolate, leaving some white streaks of egg white for a marbled appearance.

★ Immediately drop the batter by rounded tablespoons onto the prepared baking sheet, spacing them about 1 inch (2.5 cm) apart.

★ Bake the cookies until dry and crisp on the outside but still soft inside, about 10 minutes. Let the cookies cool on the baking sheet on a wire rack for 10 minutes, then gently transfer them to wire racks to cool completely. Store in an airtight container at room temperature for up to 5 days.

Makes about 20 cookies

S'more Love

Spread s'more love! Share these yummy brownies—inspired by America's favorite campfire dessert—with your loved ones and make your world a better place.

Ingredients

1 cup (8 oz/250 g) unsalted butter

10 ounces (315 g) bittersweet chocolate, finely chopped

1 cup (8 oz/250 g) granulated sugar

¾ cup (6 oz/185 g) light brown sugar, firmly packed

4 large eggs

2 teaspoon pure vanilla extract

1 teaspoon kosher salt

1⅓ cups (5½ oz/170 g) cake flour

3 tablespoons natural cocoa powder

About 6 graham crackers, roughly crumbled

About 12 jumbo marshmallows

Candy-coated chocolates, for topping

★ Preheat oven to 350°F (180°C). Generously butter a 9-by-13-inch (23-by-33-cm) baking dish.

★ In a saucepan, melt the butter and chocolate over low heat, stirring often, about 4 minutes. Remove from the heat and whisk in the brown sugar and the granulated sugar. Whisk in the eggs one at a time, beating well after each addition. Whisk in the vanilla and salt.

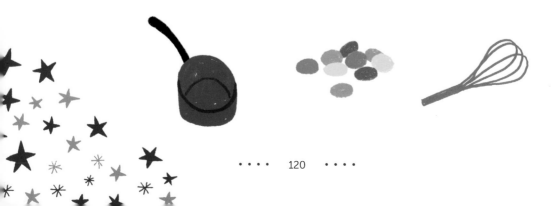

★ Sift the flour and cocoa over the chocolate mixture and, using a rubber spatula, stir until just blended. Fold in the graham crackers. Pour into the prepared dish and spread evenly. Top with the marshmallows.

★ Bake until a toothpick inserted into the center comes out almost completely clean, 30–35 minutes. Let cool in the dish on a wire rack, then cut into 12 large squares and top with red and blue candy-coated chocolates.

Makes 12 brownies

About the ACLU

We mentioned in our introduction that we donated 100 percent of the proceeds from our Bake America Great Again bake sale to the ACLU, but we hadn't known much about its founding until this project. In the aftermath of World War I, uneasy and fearful years in world history, the United States saw a rise in racism and the violation of civil rights. People who spoke out in the name of justice were brutalized and arrested by the thousands, often without warrants. A small group of people decided they couldn't stand what was happening, so they formed the American Civil Liberties Union with the purpose of fighting back.

Today, the ACLU has more than three hundred staff and thousands of volunteer attorneys working tirelessly on behalf of all American citizens. If you find that the freedoms to which you're entitled have been violated or that your constitutional rights have been undermined, the ACLU wants to know about it. And its team will work, free of charge, in pursuit of justice. Causes the ACLU works for include: equal rights for women, equal rights for LGBQT people, equal voting rights, equal workplace rights, equal rights for all ethnicities, equal rights for those with disabilities, religious freedom, academic freedom, protection of immigrants, and protection of our environment. Nonprofit and nonpartisan, the ACLU operates without the assistance of government funding. Its work is paid for by member dues, contributions, and grants.

When we hosted our Bake America Great Again sale—our first effort at rolling up our sleeves in the name of making a difference—we knew the ACLU would be the perfect beneficiary of our profits. We are grateful to be working with a publisher who has committed to contributing part of the proceeds from the sale of this book to the ACLU (which means that, having made a purchase, you too have made a difference). There are many worthy organizations around the country doing important work in our communities—choose one you believe in and support it in any way you can.

Bake Sales: An American Tradition

What we didn't realize as we organized our bake sale was that we were harkening back to the roots of charitable giving in our country. Have you ever wondered how the bake sale originated? We sure didn't. Yet somewhere in our memory was ingrained the idea that a bake sale was a way we could help meet the needs of others and create social change.

As it turns out, bake sales in America began in the 1800s as a fundraising strategy appropriate to the cultural constructs of the time. Women were expected to excel in the domestic sphere and were keepers of hearth and home. It was considered inappropriate for middle-and upper-class women to enter into the public sector, but through bakes sales and other charity-based events they functionally built businesses in which they operated as accountants, investors, and executives. They produced goods, raised and managed funds, and created annual reports, and their endeavors funded schools, churches, charities, and even supplies for soldiers during the Civil War.

Over time, by caring for others and for the causes they were passionate about, women were able to build support for a goal that would empower them beyond anything they had achieved thus far: they began to argue passionately for women's suffrage. And through the influence of these activists, laws and the culture changed.

We can follow in the footsteps of these trailblazing women and pursue a cause with passion, in the process creating massive social change. The journey toward becoming a great country for all has been a long one, marked by progress forward and steps back and encompassing many different strategies for bringing about change. But the humble bake sale remains—a delicious, grassroots, community-engaging, joy-inducing way to support and fund the causes we believe in. We need to remember that we all have the power to create social change. Sometimes it is necessary that we make a speech, but we should also remember it is sometimes as powerful to make a cake.

Show Off Stars-and-Stripes Style

Whether you're holding a bake sale, having a party or a summer barbecue, making after-school snacks, or just baking up sweet treats for family and friends, pretty details make all the difference.

SET A PATRIOTIC SCENE

Decorate your space to reflect your theme of liberty, justice, and the pride we all take in our American institutions. The key to making patriotic decor work is to start with a neutral base. From there, you can take your decor in any direction—breezy Southern style, urban chic, or homespun charm. What look are you going for? Think about that before you begin decorating!

★ For a bright, daytime event: Invest in a thick, white tablecloth and white plates and platters. Now your baked goods can really shine. The icing and sprinkles will become the main event! Top your treats with tiny flags and bake muffins and cupcakes in red, white, and blue paper liners. Set out tiny chalkboards labels for each sweet or display one larger chalkboard with a list. Sprinkle colored glitter stars on the corner of the table. Or contain the glitter in small glass jars and mingle them among the goods.

★ For a sleek, nighttime event: If you're looking to set an evening mood, begin with black. A dark base will make the bold red, white, and blue really pop. Wrap your baked goods in parchment paper with a single bold-colored ribbon or oversized graphic sticker. Use tiered cake stands to display your sweets, and top items with single, colorful candies. Accent the room with gold and silver stars, perhaps hanging them from the ceiling in small groupings. Tent thick, gold card-stock labels in front of each offering, and use letter stamps to spell out each name. Fly a flag behind your table to salute those stars and stripes!

★ For an event with a homespun feel: Work with earthy tones found in twine and burlap. Think layers! Use a tablecloth with thin ticking stripes as your base, and overlay with canvas or burlap. Go with creamy off-white lace or bunting to decorate, and display your baked goods in wicker baskets. Tie jars of cookies with twine, and line baskets with red and blue cloth. Handwrite labels on cream-colored card stock to identify each baked good and display them in tiny gold or wooden frames. Plant flags around the base of your table (and don't be surprised if people ask to take them home).

PERFECT PRESENTATION

The recipes in this book are delectable on their own, but add a little packaging magic and display pizazz, and they'll be downright irresistible. Whether you are offering your treats for sale, displaying them at a party, or sharing them as gifts, dress them in their best before you send them out into the world!

10 Sweet Packaging Ideas

1. Secure parchment paper wrapping with decorative washi tape.
2. Make envelopes for items from flag-themed wrapping paper.
3. Fold doilies around treats and tie with ribbon.
4. Fill cardboard boxes with candy and use as cake pop stands.
5. Use paper CD envelopes for cookie bags.
6. Label jars with eye-catching stickers.
7. Tie cellophane bags with curled ribbons.
8. Fasten disposable forks to items with twine.
9. Affix mini "love note" messages to items.
10. Set cupcakes in painted egg cartons by the dozen.

10 Decorative Flourishes for a Table

1. Hang stars-and-stripes streamers like bunting.
2. Arrange red, white, and blue flowers in simple vases.
3. Set out framed sayings that capture the spirit of your event.
4. Label baked goods with printed, tented cards.
5. Mix and match items on tiered trays and platters, to add height and visual interest.
6. Stack different-shaped red, white, and blue boxes to serve as platforms for your treats.
7. Bring levity with patriotic balloons.
8. Group flags of varying sizes in small glasses.
9. Wrap beautiful bunting around table legs or base.
10. Use painted or patterned clothespins to hang signs from twine.

Index